Working with Parents
Makes Therapy Work

Working with Parents Makes Therapy Work

Kerry Kelly Novick
and Jack Novick

Jason Aronson
Lanham • Boulder • New York • Toronto • Oxford

Published in the United States of America
by Jason Aronson
An imprint of Rowman & Littlefield Publishers, Inc.

A wholly owned subsidiary of
The Rowman & Littlefield Publishing Group, Inc.
4501 Forbes Boulevard, Suite 200, Lanham, Maryland 20706
www.rowmanlittlefield.com

PO Box 317
Oxford
OX2 9RU, UK

British Library Cataloguing in Publication Information Available

Library of Congress Cataloging-in-Publication Data

Novick, Kerry Kelly.
    Working with parents makes therapy work / Kerry Kelly Novick and Jack Novick.
        p. cm.
    Includes bibliographical references and index.
    ISBN 0-7657-0107-3 (cloth : alk. paper)
    1. Child psychotherapy—Parent participation. 2. Adolescent psychotherapy—
Parent participation. 3. Child analysis. 4. Adolescent analysis. 5. Parent and child.
I. Novick, Jack. II. Title.

RJ505.P38N685 2005
618.92'8914—dc22   2004021080

Printed in the United States of America

♾™ The paper used in this publication meets the minimum requirements of American
National Standard for Information Sciences—Permanence of Paper for Printed Library
Materials, ANSI/NISO Z39.48-1992.

With love, respect, and gratitude for their friendship and teaching, we dedicate this book to the memory of Erna Furman and Robert Furman.

CONTENTS

ACKNOWLEDGMENTS

Writing acknowledgments for a book is usually left to the last. It is a most pleasurable task, but also difficult as there are so many people to thank. We will start with our students at the Michigan Psychoanalytic Institute, the New York Freudian Society, the Michigan Psychoanalytic Council, and the New York University Psychoanalytic Institute. The difficulties our students and colleagues encountered in starting and engaging child and adolescent patients in treatment turned our attention to systematic and theoretical difficulties in work with parents. The subsequent success of our students when applying some of our ideas spurred us on—for this we are very grateful.

Early versions of the ideas presented in this book were presented across the country and in Europe; we would like to thank colleagues (who often became friends) for being so encouraging and for providing us with opportunities for stimulating exchange. In particular we would like to thank Enrico DeVito of Milan who not only invited us to speak, but also gave us insight into different forms of parent-child relationships. Andreas Giannakoulis of Rome and Veikko Aalberg and others in Finland helped us expand our ideas.

In the United States we especially want to acknowledge the encouragement of Janis Baeuerlen and the enthusiastic group of child analysts, therapists, and candidates of the San Francisco Psychoanalytic Institute. Kirkland Vaughns, the editor of the innovative *Journal of Infant, Child, and Adolescent Psychotherapy*, published earlier versions of this work, as did Jer-

ACKNOWLEDGMENTS

rold Brandell in the *Journal of Psychoanalytic Social Work*. Numerous colleagues challenged and encouraged us, among them Judith Chused and Erna Furman who wrote helpful and thought-provoking critiques of our earlier drafts. Art Farley, James Herzog, Arthur Rosenbaum, Sam Rubin, and others discussed our presentations at scientific sessions of the American Psychoanalytic Association meetings, and we always came away stimulated and enriched.

We are very grateful to the families, staff, and volunteers at Allen Creek Preschool for keeping us focused on finding words to communicate and ways to test the relevance and efficacy of our ideas.

We thank our children, Rebecca, Ben, and Anna, for all that we have learned and experienced about the joys, challenges, and transformative possibilities of parenthood.

CHAPTER ONE
PARENT WORK—INTRODUCTION
AND HISTORY

A Work in Progress

The description of parent work that follows in this book is an evolving model. It comes from long years of struggling with some treatments that never got started or that were interrupted or terminated suddenly or prematurely. We were not trained to work as we describe in this book, but over the years we saw that many of our difficulties, and those of our colleagues and students, stemmed in part from the lack of a clear model for clinical work with parents of child or adolescent patients.

Parents of children or adolescents usually seek an evaluation at a point of urgency. They feel frustrated, guilty, and angry. They have exhausted other remedies and come to the therapist looking for answers, solutions, and absolution. There is intense pressure to see the child and fix the problem. There is a correspondingly intense pull within therapists to respond to a family's distress by jumping in to help—acceding to the parents' treatment plan and initiating therapy immediately with the child. Too often this approach results in early treatment failure and withdrawal.

It seems to us that the major test of any psychoanalytic concept and the techniques that follow from it resides in the clinical situation. Is it helpful or not? We have found that our work with children and adolescents, and that of our colleagues and students, is more effective when parent work is included in the overall structure of the treatment.

1

CHAPTER ONE

The Tasks and Problems of Clinical Work

The practical task of clinical work with young people is to get the child or adolescent into treatment, do the therapeutic work, and finish in a timely fashion. There are many factors in the patient that affect this process. Equally, there are many factors in parents that help or interfere. Other aspects of circumstances or history, such as adoption, divorce, blended or differently structured families, illness, death, handicap, and so forth, have greater or lesser effects on the developing personality and health of the child.

There are relatively well-articulated theories and techniques for work with children and adolescents. But many therapies never get started or are interrupted or terminated suddenly. A major reason is the lack of a clear model for clinical work with parents in conjunction with their child's therapy. There is little agreement about the extent of the work, who should do it, what the goals are, and how to organize and structure it.

Parent work has a long and checkered history in psychoanalysis. It is largely an unofficial history, for many reasons. The first child analysis (S. Freud 1909) was conducted via the parent, and a close study of one of Anna Freud's earliest cases reveals the extent to which she did parent work as part of her treatment of the school-aged Peter Heller in the 1920s (Heller 1990). Yet when writing on child analysis and therapy, analysts often either ignore parent work or relegate it to a minor function, such as the gathering of information (Glenn, Sabot, and Bernstein 1978). In a seminal paper, Rosenbaum (1994) discusses current practice in the evaluation of children. He notes the "absence of clear technical guidelines for work with parents" (Rosenbaum 1994, 467). This conclusion is reaffirmed in Linda Hirshfeld's (2001) important study of the literature and the practice of parent work in child analysis and child psychotherapy. She states, "The question of parent work in child analysis and therapy has been a subject of controversy and, although it is a lively topic of discussion, it has remained relatively neglected and inconspicuous in the literature" (Hirshfeld 2001, 7).

Resistances to Parent Work

It is worth considering possible causes for the history of relative neglect of parent work, since the determinants may continue to influence both the-

2

ory and technique adversely. We would group the reasons under *social/historical*, *theoretical*, *political*, and *psychodynamic* headings.

Social/Historical

The social/historical reasons relate to the role of Western women in the second half of the nineteenth and beginning of the twentieth centuries. Women tended to be idealized but at the same time stripped of any overt power, including sexual power. This ambivalent sociocultural attitude toward women, especially mothers, inevitably colored the assumptions of the psychoanalytic pioneers. It is clearly seen, for instance, in Freud's adolescent letters to Silberstein (Boelich 1990) and in his understanding of the case of "Little Hans" (S. Freud 1909). In this work, Freud has nothing but praise for the boy's mother, even though she is the one who constantly threatens the boy with castration if he continues to masturbate. The mother is not seen as having much impact on the child's development except as an object of desire and thus an occasion of rivalry with the father. It is the *father's* threat that combines with the boy's developmental desires to produce what Freud termed the Oedipus complex. This occurs relatively late in the child's life, so the role of the preoedipal mother is denied.

Theoretical

With the failure of his seduction hypothesis, Freud (1897) made a decisive turn from external reality, which would include the effect of the parents, to intrapsychic wishes and desires as the prime determinants of neuroses. This change in theoretical focus seems to be a major reason for the relative neglect of parent work. The shift to the internal world was reinforced by a theory of development that emphasized endogenous unfolding of psychosexual phases independent of environmental influences. So once again, with the support of psychoanalytic theory, the past and current impact of parents could be denied. Close reading of Freud's writings reveals that his practice was usually to integrate theoretical changes rather than to reject earlier formulations and replace them with newer ideas. Many of his followers, however, tended to embrace new theories to the exclusion of previous ones. They tended to use the changes in theory to justify ignoring the role of parents in the treatment of children.

CHAPTER ONE

Political

Demonstrating the Equality between Child and Adult Work

Although child observation and the developmental point of view were at the core of psychoanalysis from the very beginning, psychoanalysis as a method of treatment for children did not start until the 1920s with the work of Anna Freud, Melanie Klein, Hermine von Hug-Hellmuth, and the Bornsteins (A. Freud 1966). These pioneers were very eager to demonstrate that child analysis followed the same principles as the most recent models of adult work, and thus they further reinforced denial of the pathogenic or constructive impact of the family. This was especially true of Melanie Klein, whose theory and technique ignored environmental effects and presented child analysis as equivalent in all respects to adult work. Modern Kleinians continue this style, as described, for instance, by Elmhirst (1988), Baruch (1997), and Pick and Segal (1978). Some early child analytic practitioners, however, were aware of the complexities of the issues surrounding parent work: von Hug-Hellmuth noted that relationships with parents, however difficult, were an inevitable part of the child's treatment and that "it is a legitimate demand on the part of the parents and furthers the treatment" (1921, 304).

Anna Freud's evolving technique of child analysis differed markedly from the Kleinian position, but in relation to parent work they both had little to say. Thus, the two most influential leaders in child analysis initially presented models of exclusively one-to-one work with child patients. Rosenbaum observed that

> other than referring parents for treatment, there is little said or written about the possibility of working with the parents in an ongoing manner, parallel with the treatment of the child, to identify and ameliorate the effect of difficulties regularly encountered. In fact, there is even reticence about discussing the details of the interactions between the analyst and the parents, perhaps because such interactions and the influence exerted through them tend to degrade the idealization of the adult analytic process. (1994, 468)

Individual Treatment of Parents as the Answer to Parenting Difficulties

These militating forces continued in the twenties and thirties as psychoanalysis evolved into the ego psychology that dominated the field for a quarter of a century after the end of the Second World War. At that point a significant shift began in a number of the factors alluded to above, but paradoxically the very success of psychoanalysis in the mid-twentieth century as the only or preeminent form of psychotherapy delayed what would have been a natural progression to a greater focus on parent work. Two trends contributed to that situation. The preeminence of ego psychology included an acceptance of and focus on child development and child psychoanalysis. But the research work of child analysts, especially that of Margaret Mahler and her colleagues (Mahler, Pine, and Bergman 1975), which could have led to increased focus on parents, had the opposite impact when her work was extensively applied to adolescents by analysts who came to this work from an adult rather than a child training and perspective. Most influential in this regard were the ideas of Masterson and Rinsley (Rinsley 1981), wherein parent work consisted of the removal of the adolescent from the dysfunctional family to "appropriate reparenting" (1981, 261) in an inpatient or residential setting. Their use of Mahler's work on separation and individuation basically cut the parents out of the treatment. This had a profound effect on a generation of adolescent therapists and entered psychoanalytic theory in the form of assumptions of normative distancing between adolescents and their parents.

Those who worked with children and adolescents in an outpatient setting also neglected parent work because of an overvaluation or idealization of the efficacy of psychoanalysis for parents. The parents of many child patients were in psychoanalysis themselves, either privately or through one of the many clinics offering psychoanalyses to both parents and children, so the special nature of work with parents could be avoided. Child analysts tended to think that parental changes would occur through analysis, a view that is still maintained by many. It was assumed that psychoanalysis would deal with parental pathology and resistances and so ensure that the child's treatment would not be interrupted. This hope was rarely borne out for several reasons.

First, adult pathology may often be sequestered in the parent-child relationship and addressed late in the patient's treatment or not at all. The focus of adult work is the entire personality of the adult patient, of which parenting is only one aspect. General change comes slowly and gradually in adult treatment and may have only indirect effects on parenting, perhaps missing out on interferences in that realm altogether, and often missing

crucial developmental years in the child's life. The issue of directly addressing parenting issues in adult analysis, with a range of practice from
giving of advice to explicit exclusion, remains controversial, as discussed,
for instance, by Kris (1981).

Second, data from research carried out at the Hampstead Clinic by
means of the simultaneous analysis of parent and child revealed, as expected, the close interrelationship of parental and child pathology. But
surprisingly, it also showed the limits of analysis as the method of parent
work, as well as how little the child often figured in the parental analysis
(Burlingham, Goldberger, and Lussier 1955; A. Freud 1965; Hellman
1960; Levy 1960; Sprince 1962). Anna Freud summarized some of these
issues when she said,

> There is a point that is not usually taken sufficiently into account by
> child analysts. With adult patients who have children, analysts see very
> clearly in analysis what a small part of the parents' personality is really
> involved with the child, and how great is the part that has nothing to do
> with the child. . . . It is quite wrong to think that because the child is so
> highly involved with the parent, the parent is equally exclusively in-
> volved with the child. (in Sandler, Kennedy, and Tyson 1980, 217)

Third, and very importantly, the special closeness of the parent-child
relationship has a powerful positive and negative impact on the child's potential progress and needs to be addressed directly. Parents themselves
have mixed feelings about their primacy with their children, wanting to
repudiate how important they are to avoid guilt and simultaneously
fiercely protecting their exclusive position as central in their children's
lives. This is a crucial arena for parent work to be discussed throughout
this book.

Fourth, the parenting function per se may be most effectively worked
on in the context of the child's treatment, where parents can be enlisted to
bring their best functioning. As we will illustrate, parents of child patients
are often more disturbed than adults who present for treatment, but they
are also capable sometimes of rising above their own difficulties for the
sake of their children.

Lastly, the extent and permanence of change in the child is almost
always dependent on parental capacity to change and to support the

child's growth. Parents may additionally need treatment in their own right. The impetus may spring from parent work, but neither replaces the other.

Interaction of Child and Adult Development— Internal and External

Early on, Sigmund Freud (1917) had written of the "complemental series," a very modern view of the interaction of innate and environmental factors. The crucial role of parents in promoting health or pathology was described in all of Freud's cases. At the end of the book that records a remarkable series of discussions at the Hampstead Clinic (Sandler et al. 1980), Anna Freud takes a similar position regarding child analysis, saying, "Therefore, in child analysis, assistance from both sides is needed— internal help for the method of coping, but external help for undue pressures on the child" (1980, 268). Foremost among these pressures from the external world were parental interferences with the child's development and treatment. In her list of the "host of disadvantages" (Sandler et al. 1980, v) to doing child analysis, Anna Freud cites "the unavoidable intrusion of parents" (1980, v).

It seems that Anna Freud retained a mixed attitude about the role of parents in child treatment to the end of her life, yet a shift from her thinking of the 1920s was visible in much of her clinical and research focus in the later years. Erna Furman noted that Anna Freud

> was thoroughly ambivalent about parents; on the one hand truly silenced those on her staff who advocated work with parents (Ruth Thomas, Lydia Jacobs, Margarete Ruben), on the other hand was in awe of those who were mothers themselves in most instances and, at times, had some real insights. It was she who told [me] "In child analysis, the analyst has to invest equally three areas—the child, the mother, and the mother-child relationship." (1998, personal communication)

Competition for Child Patients

The current, early twenty-first-century shift in public perception of and third-party payment for psychoanalysis has made it increasingly difficult to obtain analytic patients in general, and child patients in particular. So attention to understanding parental resistances to treatment is further spurred by the competition for child patients among the many seemingly easier and quicker solutions available, such as medication or behavioral contracting. Parents were first ignored; then, in the halcyon days of psychoanalysis, they were explicitly excluded or taken for granted; and now, in the struggle with the array of apparently simpler solutions, parents are seen as the main interference with the start, maintenance, or appropriate ending of analysis. Despite this fact, work with parents is still a topic little written about, discussed, or conceptualized by child psychoanalysts. In a survey of all child analytic training programs of the American Psychoanalytic Association, only one out of twenty-two attributed the decrease in child patients to a neglect of training in parent work (Committee on Child and Adolescent Analysis, 1997). So the continuing neglect may be due in part to the fact that child treatment and parent work are thought of as "second class psychotherapy" (Chethik 1989, 239), an "inferior type of professional occupation" (A. Freud 1970, 211).

Dynamic

We have discussed so far the external factors that contribute to resistance to child analysis in general and parent work in particular. But many of these external factors have changed—yet the resistance persists. As analysts we turn then to consideration of unconscious factors, which are timeless issues from the beginning of psychoanalysis. Currently, most child analysts would probably agree that work with parents is important in some degree to effective child analysis. They would differ, however, over the aims and techniques of such work. Implicit in the controversy is the continuing need experienced by most child analysts to demonstrate that the work they do is indeed psychoanalysis and not a watered-down form of psychotherapy, as has been asserted by some adult analysts, notably Brenner (1985). As in the beginning of child analysis, the model aspired to has tended to remain a classical adult one. In this model, current external reality is mostly irrelevant and can even be deemed to pose a threat to the undistorted unfolding of transference and the psychoanalytic process (Rosenbaum 1994).

Restoration to the Path of Progressive Development

After the Second World War, Anna Freud began to evolve a view of development and treatment that soon became a rather radical but consistent extension of psychoanalytic theory and technique. It went beyond the contemporary psychoanalytic model that had not then proceeded much further than Freud's technical papers of 1912 and 1913. Of particular importance was Anna Freud's concept of "restoration to the path of progressive development" (1965) as the overarching treatment goal. There are currently many writers addressing the ways in which psychoanalysis can be an important developmental experience in itself (Emde 1988a, 1988b; Hurry 1998; Meissner 1996; J. Novick 1990; Tahka 1993).

The years from 1945 were years of creative ferment for Anna Freud and many other child analysts, but the implications of their contributions were denied or ignored by analysts of adults and limited to child work by child analysts themselves. Anna Freud was addressing issues that would arise much later for adult analysts confronted by challenges from object-relations theorists, self psychologists, separation and attachment theorists, interaction and intersubjective models, and the adult fascination with enactment. However, she held back from applying her views to adult analysis, as did other child analysts. She and other child analysts seemed to remain under the thrall of the adult psychoanalytic model, a constraint that interfered with the development of a general theory of child analysis, including a theory of work with parents.

Child Analysis as a Foundation for an Inclusive Psychoanalytic Theory and Technique

Anna Freud's work was seldom referred to within ten years after her death. In 1990, we wrote about child analysis being like the youngest child in the family, desperately trying to emulate the older children and inevitably falling short (J. Novick 1990). We wondered then what psychoanalytic technique would have looked like if Freud's first patients had been children and adolescents rather than adults. We listed a number of plausible differences, foremost among them being the centrality of the role of parents in the treatment. If child analysts had felt less diffident about stressing the importance of child analytic experience, perhaps the child analytic literature would be included in the mainstream to the benefit of a more balanced perspective on the relative importance of fantasy and reality, internal and external, and past and present in the theory of psychoanalysis and technique (K. K. Novick and J. Novick 2002c).

Gender Issues for Child Analysts

There seems to be a diffidence in child analysts to presenting their work as fundamental to a general theory of psychoanalysis. Sigmund Freud was a champion of child analysis, as was Sandor Ferenczi. Both men were comfortable placing child analysis at the center of psychoanalytic theory and technique. But the female pioneers, especially Anna Freud, seemed to have had a passive-submissive relationship to the psychoanalytic fathers. In an introduction to Anna Freud's classic 1922 paper about beating fantasies and daydreams, we noted her own lifelong struggle with a fixed beating fantasy and concluded that she had

> a general quality of sometimes drawing back at the last minute, as if she did not truly trust or believe in the power of her own thinking or in her political standing within psychoanalysis. It was as if she continually compromised between the beating fantasy and gratification through real effectance. (K. K. Novick and J. Novick 1999, 68–69)

In that introduction we described Anna Freud's submission to her father and her inability to integrate the importance of the preoedipal mother into her theories. It is in relation to the imagined omnipotence of the pregendered Ur-mother of infancy that we perceive the deepest and most persistent resistances to work with parents. Erna Furman contributed enormously to understanding the development of parent-child relationships and their role in child treatment. She also addressed what she saw as fundamental resistances within analysts themselves to engaging with early mother-child issues. In other words, she identified a dynamic interference with the integration of parent work into the therapeutic repertoire. In response to our papers on parent work (J. Novick and K. K. Novick 2001, 2002b; K. K. Novick and J. Novick 2002a, 2002b), Erna Furman wrote that the reasons for neglect of parent work "lie, of course, in the need to be the mother, even the better mother, and this then necessitates all kinds of reactions of a defensive nature to the mother who might assert herself or to those who speak up for her. It is a very touchy topic" (1998, personal communication; see also E. Furman [1996] on parenting the hospitalized child).

Role of Rescue Fantasies in the Clinician— Hostility to Parents

We have found that many child workers, including child analysts, may be driven by rescue fantasies, which places the dynamics of the phenomenon within a system of mental functioning that uses a hostile omnipotent fantasy as a defense against helplessness. The unconscious hostility to parents contained in the therapist's fantasy of rescuing the child may be the element of response to parents' defensive hostility that contributes to the difficulty of the work. In order to feel with parents, especially the mother, the child analyst must become aware of his or her own unconscious primitive wishes, fears, and defensive and reactive rage to the "pregendered" mother, the first object of identification for both boys and girls (Furman 1997). Current psychoanalytic literature tends to emphasize early gender differentiation, phallic narcissistic comparisons, and the sexual and parental roles of the oedipal phase, but we would agree with Furman that core identity is formed first with a nongendered mother. Furman (1997, 126) emphasizes the "flexible body boundaries" of the mother and notes that this can be a source of primitive anxiety for both the mother and those she relates to. We have noted in our work on the determinants of sadomasochism that attachment through psychical or physical pain to the early mother can become the core experience for later pathology (K. K. Novick and J. Novick 1987.) It is no wonder, then, that all those who work with children are vulnerable to reacting to and defending against the Ur-mother. This must be acknowledged, shared, and worked through before effective parent work can be done.

We have noticed a related phenomenon in training child analysts, particularly female candidates contemplating starting child cases. If they are parents themselves, there is often a reluctance to treat a child near the age of their own child. This attitude is often acceded to without question, but we wonder why it does not appear that candidates set any such limits when taking on an adult case. We think there is an assumption that any counterreactions to adult patients will be addressed in their own analysis and supervision, but they lack such confidence in relation to child work. Child analytic candidates have told us that they worried that work with the *parents* of child patients would stir up feelings about their own parenting that they would not be able to handle.

Doubts about Using Feelings—Counterreactions

There are additional dynamic sources of analysts' resistance to parent work. Modern psychoanalytic training for work with adults incorporates the analyst's feelings as useful data in clinical work. Because of historical/political avoidance of work with parents, child analysts have not been supported in similarly working to understand and use their feelings in the work with children or their parents. Trainees are rarely supported in encompassing and addressing the emotional intensity of contact with parents and the revival of very early mother-child longings, experiences, and conflicts. One result is defensive constraint and formulaic application of technique. Many students of child analysis complete their training after the end of their personal analyses, which leaves them without the most important resource for understanding their own reactions. Thus there can be an institutionalized denial of the reality that work with parents may be a most demanding clinical situation for any analyst.

Clinician's Transferences and Reactions to Parents

Child analysts meet with a mother and a father. This is bound to evoke a transference response at many levels in the analyst, including the most primitive vulnerabilities, as discussed above. In addition, unlike adults who present themselves for evaluation or treatment, parents are assessing the real person of the analyst as someone to whom they are potentially going to entrust their child. They respond to the child analyst not only as a transference object but also as a real person. They are appropriately motivated by a wish to protect their child, rather than to protect the analyst from criticism or judgment. In this situation, the analyst feels further exposed and vulnerable, prone to invoke his or her own defenses.

Knowledge about Parent Work Exists

This discussion of the complex history of parent work in child analysis and therapy shows that there is still much to understand. In the meantime, child workers continue to struggle in the day-to-day work of helping children and parents. Signposts have been available throughout the development of psychoanalytic theory and technique over the last hundred years, but myriad resistances have made them difficult for many to follow. Despite the important efforts of psychoanalytic pioneers and more recent significant contributions by Erna Furman and her coworkers, Chethik (1989), Rosenbaum (1994), Siskind (1997), Hirshfeld (2001), and our work on the therapeutic alliance with parents, little has changed. In 1999, the *International Journal of Psycho-Analysis* published a letter from Erna Furman in response to an account of a failed treatment of a five-year-old boy (Baruch 1997). She said,

> It is sad to read about the suffering inflicted on a child analyst, his young patient, and the patient's parents, all resulting from ignorance of the role of parents in all aspects of a child's life, including his analysis. And, even as this distressing experience prompts the analyst to become more aware of the parents' feelings and of needed changes in relating with and helping them, one is saddened to realize that such a baptism by fire was needed when, in fact, answers were at hand all along. (E. Furman 1999, 172)

We have additionally noted that even therapists who know the literature and have been taught the importance of parent work sometimes still fail to act on that knowledge when appropriate. This was illustrated in the premature ending of a thirteen-year-old in treatment with a junior colleague.

> An analyst was treating a thirteen-year-old boy suffering from various phobic symptoms. His mother was deeply troubled and overly enmeshed in her son's physical and emotional life. She attended regular parent sessions, but spent much of the time on her own anxieties. The therapist felt assailed by this material and resentful of the mother's lack of focus on her child. She also recognized that this woman needed treatment of her own and suggested referring her to a colleague, without assuring her of their continued work together. A week later, the mother sat passively by in a parent session while the father declared his unilateral decision to end the treatment. In retrospect it seemed certain that the mother felt rejected and betrayed by the analyst and struck back by leaving her.

CHAPTER ONE

The Deepest Resistance

Working with parents in the way we will describe in this book is not easy
for us, and we doubt that it could be for anyone. There are many reasons
for this—we detailed above some of the historical, theoretical, social, and
political ones. But the main resistance surely comes from the deep and intense countertransferences to parents that we all struggle with. Thus we
are often aware in ourselves of defensiveness, avoidance, awkwardness,
procrastination, and so forth in trying to implement our own model. As in
all things psychoanalytic, this model is a work in progress. We will next
describe our fundamental assumptions and, in the chapters that follow, illustrate technical interventions with parents of patients of all ages through
the phases of treatment from evaluation to posttermination.

CHAPTER TWO
OUR ASSUMPTIONS WHEN
WE WORK WITH PARENTS

E very model of therapeutic activity and therapeutic action rests on explicit or implicit assumptions. In this chapter we will describe the underlying thinking that shapes our work with parents in the context of clinical and theoretical ideas that guide our work in general.

Parenthood Is a Normal Adult Developmental Phase

Throughout this work there is an underlying assumption that parenthood is a normal adult developmental phase. As we understand and use this idea, the phase of parenthood signifies the capacity to create, care for, protect, nurture, love, respect, and take pleasure in something or someone beyond the self. As such, it does not necessarily imply bearing and rearing children, although that is the context of our present discussion.

We emphasize that development is not a force confined to childhood, ending in adolescence, but that it continues throughout the life cycle and includes the powerful postadolescent phase of parenthood (Benedek 1959; E. Furman 1969; J. Novick 1990). K. Novick (1988) has described the important dynamic distinction in little girls between childbearing and child rearing. Here we are stressing the postadolescent task of uniting the two strands of development so that parenthood goes beyond childbearing to the more important and long-term task of child rearing. The confluence of current cultural and socioeconomic influences has added to the complexity for women in merging these two dimensions of development, with a resulting overemphasis on childbearing as the defining marker of parenthood (Leon 1997, 1998). We assume, however, that child rearing is the core of the psychological phase of parenthood. Regardless of cultural or psychological interferences, there seems to be in each individual a need to create something beyond the self—to be a psychological parent.

Within the phase of parenthood, there are subphases that correlate with levels of children's development. Parents on a progressive developmental path show flexibility and integration of subphases; others struggle with fixations and conflicts over core tasks within subphases and their interaction with conflicts and tasks of mastery in children.

Parents and Children Are Involved in a Lifelong Complex Interaction

The interaction of child development and parental functioning has been a fundamental tenet of psychoanalysis since the beginning. This axiom appears in some form in every major psychoanalytic school of thought. We apply this basic idea to considering the mutually interactive development of children and parents, assuming that members of a family influence each other consciously and unconsciously throughout the life span, including grandparenthood, old age, and death, to both constructive and pathological effect.

The nature of the internalized parent representation and the mental relationship with internalized parents have profound effects on adult functioning. Artists know this and use this fact to important dramatic effect. In the play *The Unexpected Man* by Yasmina Reza (1999), the woman describes the hospitalization and death of her friend Serge: he was a powerful, influential man, a grandfather in his seventies. When he went to the hospital he took a passport photo of his dead mother "to keep him safe." In *Good Morning Midnight*, Chip Brown (2003) describes the suicide of a sixty-seven-year-old mountain climber who wrote that he was killing himself to avoid suffering the indignities and limitations of old age. He was praised by many for his extraordinary life achievement and bravery in death, but the author presents a portrait of a person who totally cut himself off from his parents in adolescence. Then he lost his own three children through death, suicide, and repudiation. The book suggests to us that without internal parents "to keep you safe" it is hard to grow old.

Starting with her early work in 1957 on treatment via the parent, Erna Furman presented a theory of parent-child relationships that is unsurpassed in its explication of their richness and complexity. Her work is summarized in her 1992 book on toddlers and their mothers and in a paper on work with parents (1995). She takes us beyond the notion of parents as the prime source of interference with therapy to a view of the parent-child relationship as "a complex overdetermined interaction in which two closely interwoven personalities complement each other in various ever-changing unconscious ways" (1995, 25). This complex interdependence and interaction continues even into adolescence and beyond. In relation to therapy, Furman states,

> The ongoing mutual narcissistic investments between parent and child matter not only at the start of therapy but have to be taken into account all along. When we disregard the parent, we leave out crucial parts of the child's self, sometimes the best parts, and when we treat the parent and disregard the child, we commit the same mistake. (1995, 27)

Dual Goals of Child and Adolescent Treatment

- Restoration of the child to the path of progressive development
- Restoration of the parent-child relationship to a lifelong positive resource for both

Anna Freud defined the goal of child analysis as restoration of the child to the path of progressive development. We have extended this idea to include a second goal: helping parents achieve the developmental phase of parenthood, that is, restoring parents to the path of progressive adult development, in which parenthood is one phase.

Our view of the parent-child relationship provides a framework for evolving a technique of parent work that encompasses both the resistances and the developmental aids to therapy. The aim of child analysis can be recast as not only the restoration of the child's progressive development but also as the restoration of the parent-child relationship that has been disrupted by pathology to its potential as a lifelong positive resource for

17

both. Thus we are mindful throughout child or adolescent treatment of these dual goals of the work.

This idea is not only an implicit assumption, but also an explicit assertion. We tell parents early in the evaluation that we have these two goals for our endeavors together. We work with this idea until it becomes an intrinsic motivation for continued treatment.

The Therapeutic Alliance as a Conceptual Framework for Ongoing Parent Work

Parents' intense wish to do right by their child, to be the best parents they can be, regardless of the degree or type of interfering pathology, is a powerful motive force for entering into a therapeutic alliance with the analyst.

The framework for discussion of parent work that we use in this book is our revised concept of the therapeutic alliance, which includes building and maintaining an alliance between therapist and parents or significant others. We will look at parental tasks for each phase of treatment for each age group, from preschool children to late-adolescents. We will apply what we learn about resistances at each phase to enhance our understanding of work with parents at subsequent phases. Consistent with our view that each phase influences and is influenced by subsequent phases, we will also apply what we have learned to techniques of psychoanalytic work with adults.

Looking at the therapeutic relationship through the lens of the therapeutic alliance explicates and operationalizes analysis as a developmental experience for both child and parents.

Phases of Treatment

We have found it useful to apply the developmental point of view to the course of treatment. It has allowed us to think of psychoanalysis in terms of phases, therapeutic tasks, and assessment of accomplishment of those tasks, that is, the outcome of therapeutic interventions at any given point in the treatment. Applying developmental concepts to the process of therapy, one can speak of phases of treatment, from the evaluation and beginning, through the middle and pretermination, to termination and follow-up. Each treatment phase has its own nuclear conflict that is experienced by everyone.

The patient's ego has the task of solving that conflict. How he or she solves it reveals particulars of the individual patient's history and current functioning. And how the analyst responds varies with the skill, training, and orientation of the individual analyst. But, as everyone is faced with the same nuclear conflicts, we can describe the therapeutic relationship in terms of the tasks that face each and every patient and each and every analyst, as well as significant other parties to the treatment, such as parents, throughout their work together. Mutual engagement around these tasks can become a major fulcrum for therapeutic change and regaining developmental momentum.

The therapeutic alliance does not constitute the whole of the therapeutic relationship, but we hope to demonstrate that it functions as a lens that helps us see how to enlist the parents of child and adolescent patients in the work of treatment, to promote growth and change in parents during the process of their child's treatment, and as a critical technical vantage point for accessing the internal parenting functions of adult patients. The model of alliance tasks gives us ways to approach intense parental resistances. There are typical parental anxieties and resistances that arise in relation to each therapeutic alliance task. We will discuss these in detail throughout the chapters of this book, but a summary table may be found in chapter 11.

The parental therapeutic alliance tasks through the different phases of treatment provide a shared arena for working on interferences with aspects of psychological parenting. Each phase of treatment presents parents with new alliance tasks whose accomplishment consolidates progressive development in the parents. Parallel with the child's internalization of the therapeutic alliance is the parents' internalization of ways of functioning that foster and maintain mutual respect, support, love, and continued growth.

Therapeutic Alliance Tasks

Parents have therapeutic alliance tasks throughout their child's treatment (for a summary of therapeutic alliance tasks for patient, therapist, and parents or significant other, see table 1 in chapter 11):

- During evaluation, the task for parents is to begin various transformations.

- At the beginning of the child's treatment, parents have the task of allowing the child to "be with" another adult, accepting physical separation.

- In the middle phase, allowing the child to work together privately with another person means integrating the child's psychological separation.

- Enjoying and validating the child's progression is the task for parents in the pretermination phase.

- During termination, parents work to mourn their own loss of the therapy, to internalize mastery of alliance tasks, and to consolidate their own development in the phase of parenthood.

- After treatment has ended, parents allow for continued growth in the child and grow with him.

Mastery and internalization of the parental therapeutic alliance tasks moves parents through subphases of parenthood. This also represents a movement toward greater open-system functioning.

Parental Movement from the "Closed" to the "Open" System of Self-Regulation Is the Overarching Criterion of Change

The transformative tasks of the therapeutic alliance, beginning in the evaluation phase, are designed to help parents gain or regain some feeling of competence as parents and love for their child as a separate person, to consolidate open-system relationships. Woven through our work with patients of all kinds and with individuals developing normally is a set of hypotheses concerning self-regulation and sources of self-esteem in everyone (J. Novick and K. K. Novick 2002a). Faced with experiences of helplessness, from whatever source, every person has to find a way to cope and feel good. These adaptations can be constructive and creative, building what we have called an "open system" of self-regulation. Alternatively and simultaneously, at any point in development, the individual has available pathological solutions based on omnipotent defenses, which we have described as a "closed system" (for a summary of open- and closed-system responses, see table 3 in chapter 11). The quality and form of love in relationships, including those between parents and between parents and child, relates to these two systems (J. Novick and K. K. Novick 2000). Mutually enhancing relationships stem from and produce open-system functioning and growth, while closed-system functioning conduces to and is reinforced by sadomasochistic patterns of relating. Thus we might characterize the goals of treatment for parents in terms of their movement out of closed-system functioning with their child to more open-system self-regulation and relationships with each other and with the child.

Parent Work Is Substantive and Legitimate. It Makes Use of the Full Repertoire of Psychoanalytic Interventions.

Developmental interference in parenting can be understood as pathology amenable to therapeutic work. It follows then that we consider it necessary and appropriate to use the full conceptual and technical repertoire from individual work with children and adults in the context of parent work. We do not define parent work negatively, that is, in terms of what it is not or what the restrictions may be. Rather, we see it as substantive, significant, and legitimate in its own right. Parent work therefore includes interventions traditionally labeled as "therapeutic," for example, analysis of defenses, verbalization, insight, reconstruction, interpretation, and the use of transference and countertransference for understanding and technique.

In addition to the traditional use of education, support, validation, modeling, facilitating, and so forth that have been staples of parent guidance, we can illustrate the relevance and utility of using the full range of techniques both by the difficulties that arise when the therapist pulls back from using these skills and, in the positive sense, when *interpretation* and *working through* are crucial to the achievement of both of the dual goals of treatment. In our experience, use of the full range of therapeutic techniques in parent work does not compete or interfere with individual therapy for parents. Indeed, parent work may lead to acceptance of a referral for individual treatment while maintaining the relationship with the child analyst for work on parenting issues. Parent work focuses on the parent-child relationship; other issues in the parents' lives are engaged with only as they have relevance to their relationship with their child. Thus we may use the full range of our skills without inhibition in the very limited and focused area of parenting, as we saw in work with the parents of Nicholas, an eight-year-old boy with severe food allergies.

> Both of Nicholas' parents struggled with depression that was intermittently severe. His otherwise loving and empathic mother tended to feel easily overwhelmed and weepy, while his father frequently expressed belligerent anxiety about anything and everything. Nicholas entered treatment with many fears and a history of underachieving and being bullied at school. With focus only on the therapeutic goal of restoring Nicholas to uninhibited use of his capacities, the therapist would have immediately referred both parents for individual treatment and kept the parent work to a minimum. These parents might have resisted such referrals at this juncture, and they could not yet comfortably allow Nicholas to have a separate relationship with the therapist.
>
> Instead, with the dual goals of treatment in mind, the analyst was able to start the child's treatment while working with the parents. In that context, the analyst gradually understood from the parent work the exquisite entwinement of the parents' anxieties with Nicholas' sense of omnipotent responsibility for their moods and his sadomasochistic relation to his own sense of physical vulnerability, played out in his interactions with schoolmates.
>
> As the parent work deepened, the alliance was strengthened, and finally Nicholas' father confided in a parent session that he feared for his son's life every time the boy left the house and so needed to keep him close. The analyst interpreted father's limiting of Nicholas' activities and consequent development of fears as father's use of his son in an effort to reduce his own anxieties. Both parents were visibly upset by this interpretation but could then accept the therapist's suggestion that the parent work could help untangle this issue as it impacted Nicholas, while an individual therapy for father could explore the roots and functions of father's general anxiety.
>
> Similarly, the toll of Nicholas' efforts to keep his mother happy at all costs could be illuminated for her, and a referral for psychotherapy and medication was made successfully. Work with both parents continued fruitfully throughout Nicholas' treatment.

CHAPTER THREE

EVALUATION

Evaluations Assess Both Child and Parents

E valuations of children, adolescents, and adults are usually done for
diagnostic purposes. When they are done by analysts or therapists
influenced by psychoanalytic ideas, the goal is to reach beyond description to a sense of the dynamic and historical factors that may be at
the root of the difficulty. In our model there are additional goals. The
evaluation is not only to assess and diagnose the child, but first to assess
the parents and to develop a working relationship with them. This turns
parents into partners who can work with the therapist to see how far they
can go in helping the child. Together, parents and analyst may reach a
point where it is clear to all concerned that there are underlying problems,
that there is more to the child's story. Then a recommendation for therapy
or analysis makes sense, as the goal of an analytic treatment is to understand what is behind the symptoms.

Transformations Begin during Evaluation

The joint task of parents and therapist in the evaluation is to *begin* a series of transformations within the parents, which will either be sufficient
in themselves or continue throughout subsequent treatment of the child.
These include working on changing

23

- guilt to usable concern,

- self-help to joint work,

- circumstantial explanations to internal meanings and motivations,

- externalizations onto the child to attunement with the child,

- parental helplessness to competence,

- despair to hopefulness,

- idealization or denigration of the child to primary parental love.

The analyst learns a great deal about the parents' personalities and the prospects for a successful working relationship from how parents respond to the task of beginning these transformations. Making a start lays the foundation for a relationship of collaboration and mutuality between therapist and parents. Progress in the transformation tasks during the evaluation can be measured by changes in parental capacity to see the child as a separate person. Only then can they feel genuine empathy with his or her distress in contrast to angry exasperation, injured vanity, or frustrated control.

The Importance of Evaluation

The evaluation phase has hitherto been somewhat neglected, often dispensed with, and rarely thought about as the crucial foundation for a successful treatment. Parents very frequently initiate contact with a request for therapy for their child, skipping over evaluation entirely. Both Furman and Rosenbaum have emphasized the importance of dealing with the anxieties and resistances of this crucial part of therapy. Furman (1995), among other issues, underlines the necessity for addressing parental guilt and harnessing it constructively, while Rosenbaum (1994) has described the long time needed to help parents see their child as a separate person with his or her own problems. We have subsumed all these issues under the rubric of the therapeutic alliance with parents. Engaging parents in the tasks of transformation is not only vital for the success of a child's treatment, but is also the crucial beginning of change in the direction of full functioning in the phase of psychological parenthood.

Parental Denial

The paucity of child and adolescent cases reported by most analytic centers is especially pronounced in relation to the preschool population. This is not because preschoolers do not manifest developmental deviation, but rather because parental denial is especially intense at this phase. Those of us who have worked or consulted in typical preschools can confirm what large-scale studies demonstrate, namely that at least 25 percent of preschoolers have problems that will not be "outgrown" but will result in impaired functioning in elementary school. Denial seems to be parents' main defense, one colluded with by pediatricians and teachers, and these parents generally do not seek professional help until pressured by schools after obvious developmental failures in midlatency or early adolescence. With pregnancy, or even before, the capacity to conceive and bear an intact, healthy, well-functioning child becomes a major source of parental self-esteem, especially for mothers. This deep involvement with the child's development may eventuate in a need to deny difficulties, because facing them causes unbearable psychic pain to the parent, or it may operate as a progressive force, serving the child's growth despite the cost to parental self-esteem. Denial is often a problem with fathers, who can be particularly reluctant to face their children's difficulties.

The Role of Fathers

The first child analysis was actually a treatment conducted through the father, the case of Little Hans (S. Freud 1909). Some analysts have emphasized the importance of the father in children's development (Abelin 1975, 1980; Burlingham 1973; Herzog 1982; Pruett 1985, 1992). But in the meager literature on parent work, there is almost no specific discussion of the vicissitudes of work with the fathers of child or adolescent patients. To some extent this reflects a continuing practical reality that many mothers are more flexibly available for appointments than are fathers. Nevertheless, we have found that fathers play a crucial role in all aspects of a child's development, including treatment outcome. Thus it is very important to include fathers in parent work somehow and examine any particular technical issues in that work.

We have noted several resistances in fathers to treatment of their child and to their involvement in the therapeutic process. One springs from fathers' underestimation of their own importance to the child, which often relates to issues in the marriage over parental primacy. A further contributor is defense against feelings of failure. Another is a denial of the internal nature of the child's difficulties in favor of blaming external circumstances, the mother, or other children, or reacting with moralistic anger over bad behavior. Fathers may feel their masculinity is assailed if their child has emotional difficulties. Despite apparent cultural changes, many men still feel that it is babyish or girlish to be emotional, have troubles, and need help. They expect their children, especially boys, to take control of themselves and "suck it up."

Woven through this book are many examples of the variety of parent work, including issues with fathers. Here, however, is an example of a simple intervention with a father that proved crucial for his son's development.

Robert started analysis at the age of three as a nonspeaker with a diagnosis of autism. He had a congenital deformity of the leg and walked with a noticeable limp. His father, a very nice giant of a man, had been shunted out of caretaking by Robert's mother and grandmother, a position he readily accepted, as he found it very difficult to connect to his damaged son. After the initial interviews, he said that he would support the treatment but that his wife alone would attend parent sessions while he focused on earning a living and taking care of their five-year-old daughter. The analyst suggested separate regular meetings with the father at a convenient time for him and made this a condition of the treatment. Robert's father accepted under pressure from his wife and desperation at his son's predicament.

The analyst used Robert's initial interest in his male therapist to convey to father how important it is for a child to have a father's love and involvement. The father hinted at and the analyst could verbalize father's pain and aversion to Robert's deformity. The father had been a champion swimmer—the therapist said that he could understand father's anxiety and focus on Robert's leg, which still required nightly splinting. "But he is more than a leg," said the analyst. "What I see is a tall, strong boy with large shoulders who will probably end up as large and strong as you are." He went on to ask the father which part of the body was more important in swimming.

Robert's father smiled broadly, thanked the analyst, and from then on remained connected to Robert through all the emotional vicissitudes of the treatment. Swimming together became a major activity; learning to swim across the pool signaled to Robert a readiness to consider finishing his treatment three years later.

Problems, Since Parents Are Not Patients

At the outset we have to acknowledge a major technical issue in work with parents. Parents are not the designated patients; they usually come because they or someone else sees the *child* as needing psychological intervention. Parents come to professionals because they feel helpless. If their response to helplessness is the invoking of feelings of hostile omnipotence, they may then feel overwhelming guilt. This in turn can lead to frantic attempts to avoid being traumatized by guilt, which may take the form of blaming others, especially the child, and then eventually the analyst, for their own failures. Given the constellation of failure, omnipotent defenses, overwhelming guilt, and externalization, how can we enlist the parents in an alliance whose aim is not only to help the child, but also to help the parents grow? Guilty parents may be apt to hear any suggestion of engaging in a process of personal change as a criticism, or conversely, become masochistically enthralled in a relationship with a wished-for omnipotent therapist, co-opting the child's treatment for their own.

Guilty and defensive, parents come to the situation feeling, consciously or unconsciously, that they may deserve to have their child taken away. To the extent that they are angry and frustrated with the child's lack of response to their efforts to ameliorate the situation, they may also wish to hand the child over, dump the child on the therapist, and get rid of the trouble and pain the child's difficulties have caused. This wish can cause further guilt that may be defended against by clinging to the child and undermining the development of his or her new relationship with the therapist. In extreme cases, this is one of the determinants of a negative therapeutic motivation (J. Novick 1980).

The Utility of the Therapeutic Alliance Framework

This constellation of conflicted and conflicting feelings can leave the analyst feeling overwhelmed. We think this may be one reason for therapists' demonstrable ambivalence about working with parents—it is hard to know where to start. The very parents who most need help often generate helplessness in the therapist, with real dangers to the therapeutic process posed by the mobilization of the analyst's defenses. An adaptive response to helplessness is to seek solutions through competence. For therapists, this means feeling effective in understanding the situation and having a repertoire of appropriate interventions to call upon.

We think that our developmentally informed revision of the concept of the therapeutic alliance expands the repertoire of therapists by suggesting additional ways to approach intense parental resistances. Parents' deep wish to do right by their child, to be the best parents they can be, regardless of the degree or type of interfering pathology, is a powerful motive force for the therapeutic alliance. The transformative tasks of the therapeutic alliance, beginning in the evaluation phase, are designed to help parents gain or regain some feeling of competence as parents and love for their child as a separate person.

The Format of an Evaluation

The traditional format of a child or adolescent evaluation has been to have one or two initial interviews with the parents, some meetings with the child, and then a final interview with the parents in which the therapist presents the results of the evaluation and the treatment recommendations. Our approach is to extend the evaluation in order to do as much as possible through working with the parents. Testing the power and limits of working via the parents is, in our experience, essential to the establishment of a therapeutic alliance with the parents. It reconfirms that parents are active partners in their child's treatment, that parents remain primary, and that therapists are not rival or substitute parents. Rather, the different adults have different functions, each essential to restoring the child to the path of progressive development.

Treatment of the child via the parent is a technique that was used by Anna Freud and others in the early days of child analysis in Vienna (A.

Freud 1966). It was elaborated and established by Anny Katan, first in Holland and then with her colleagues in Cleveland (Furman and Katan 1969). Development of this powerful procedure with preschoolers continues at the Hanna Perkins Center in Cleveland, and clinical illustrations abound in the journal *Child Analysis*. Modifications and variations are used by others such as Rosenbaum (1994), and we have increasingly found it to be an essential part of the evaluation process for all ages, not only preschoolers. The value of placing these powerful techniques within the framework of the therapeutic alliance is to allow the inclusion of the additional goal of restoring *parents* to the path of progressive development.

The First Phone Call

Working via the parent or working with the parent can start as early as the first phone call. We always make sure that we have at least twenty to thirty minutes available for an initial conversation with a parent who has called. We ask the parent if it is convenient to spend some time talking on the phone. Most parents welcome the opportunity to talk a bit right away, as they have called a therapist at a moment of great anxiety or frustration. There are various reasons for taking care and time at this point, and we hope thereby to accomplish a number of things. First of all, it conveys our interest and respect for what the parent is worried about and makes it clear that we want to listen. We ask the parent if they would like to tell us a bit about their concerns, why they are calling just now. This allows for immediate assessment of whether there is a situation so urgent that it demands immediate transfer to an emergency room. There is also the question of whether it is a referral appropriate for a psychotherapist or psychoanalyst, or whether other services might first be indicated. For example, a mother who calls with concerns about severe delays in language development may benefit first from immediate advice to pursue a hearing or speech and language evaluation before continuing with addressing the psychological/emotional dimensions of the difficulties.

When parents describe what is worrying them about the child's functioning, or what the school has reported, it allows us to respond in terms of taking them seriously and complimenting their effort to take good care of their child by investigating whether there is a problem. This speaks directly to the ambivalence and guilt that are inevitable when parents have reached the point of calling a therapist. We reassure parents that therapy is not a foregone conclusion, but rather that an evaluation of the situation will help them determine how best to meet their child's needs. The message is always that parents are in charge.

We describe a stepped process: it begins with parents filling out a developmental history form and returning it to us before the first meeting (the developmental history form we use can be found at the end of chapter 11). With preschool or school-aged children, we ask parents to fill out the form. With adolescents, we ask parents to do it with their child. In divorce situations, each parent is asked to complete a form. The request to complete this simple form—which can be faxed, mailed, or e-mailed—has several aims. We note to parents that the information provides us both with a beginning context, starts us thinking about the child, and thus may save time and money. When we meet for the first time, there is then already a shared knowledge base—analyst and parents are, in a sense, not strangers. It lets parents know that we assume they have the important knowledge about their own child. It conveys that the past is meaningful in understanding what is going on. And it demonstrates that the therapist is interested in the whole child, not just the current difficulties.

The plan for the evaluation is discussed in detail. The first meetings are described as an effort to learn more details about the current concerns, how they arose, and what parents and others have attempted in dealing with them. We note that therapist and parents are bound to begin to pick up patterns as they talk, to formulate questions and hypotheses, and to generate together some ideas for the parents to try out in relation to the issues. The implicit message is one of collaboration.

Practical arrangements for the first meetings are spelled out in detail, with an effort to find mutually convenient times as a further mark of respect for the parents' own lives and responsibilities. If parents do not ask, we bring up and specify the fee for each session so that there should be no surprises or misunderstandings. Knowing that parents coming for the first time to a therapist's office will be anxious, we are careful to give clear, detailed directions and instructions for the door, the waiting room, the length of the session, and so forth.

First Meetings

Once the meetings have begun, the work can move in a number of differ-ent directions. The limits of parental effectiveness may be reached quickly, or the parents may have sought help having already exhausted all the pos-sibilities open to them. But in some cases, working via the parent may continue for some time and may be sufficient to restore progressive devel-opment in child and parents. Sometimes we can predict which cases will or will not respond well to initial work via parents, but often we have been surprised at how much can be accomplished. This may be partly related to the traditional mental set, conveyed in training and in much of the pro-fessional literature, which underestimates or even omits the importance of parents in treatment of children of all ages. The gains of attempting to ac-complish therapeutic goals by the most conservative and economical means—that is, through first working via the parents—are many, whether parent work proves to be the precursor to a child's own treatment or to be all that is necessary to restore the momentum of development.

> George's parents called seeking an evaluation because their four-year-old son wanted to dress up in his older sister's clothes. George had been do-ing this for a year, but his parents had been advised by the pediatrician to ignore the behavior, as he would "grow out of it." The telephone call was prompted by the concern expressed at George's nursery school, where the teachers noted that he avoided playing with the boys and was beginning to be teased by classmates. The parents were confused and anxious, not knowing how to respond to the "feminine" behavior.
>
> The parents had taken George to a number of psychological and med-ical specialists without any definitive answers. Endocrine specialists had determined that there was no physiological disorder underlying the be-havior. George had told his parents that he wanted to be a girl and that he dressed up because it made him feel "so good." George's parents wanted the analyst to evaluate the reasons, to see George and tell them whether George was "a boy pretending to be a girl or a girl in a boy's body."
>
> The analyst suggested to the parents that he would like to meet with them first to explore George's history and see if together they could be-gin to make sense of the mystery. They came to regular sessions, with-out George, for six months. During this time it emerged first that George said clearly that he knew he was a boy but that he felt it would

31

be safer to be a girl. As they explored George's development to find out what might feel so dangerous, a serious medical history emerged.

George had undergone a series of three major surgeries to address a cranial/sacral fusion, starting at the age of nine months, with a further operation projected for age nine. In the first few meetings, the analyst provided a space for the parents to express their intense sadness and anxiety. They said they had never been able to talk about these issues with the many medical personnel who had taken care of their son.

The operations themselves had been frightening, and after each one they had to restrain George and prevent any gross motor activity. Both parents worried about George's future, and his father, who was a former star high school wrestler and football player, said with great sorrow that George would never be able to play contact sports. This work led quickly to the realization that they believed and conveyed the idea to George that being a boy exposed him to serious danger, since boys are drawn to rough sports. As they understood this, they became able to more easily separate this idea from their love for him as the boy he was. They talked to George about how they would work together with the doctors to help him stay safe from injury. They noted that he would be able to do all sorts of things that big boys liked, such as running and swimming.

Clarifying the history of the medical interventions and the prognosis with the analyst gave the parents practice in how to talk with George about the scary things that had happened when he was a baby and how to give him appropriate explanations of his condition. George then told them he could remember being held down and restrained. He recalled his frustration, terror, and rage and revealed that he felt he was being punished for being a bad boy. When the analyst wondered if George might be making any additional connections between the surgeries and the dangers of being a boy, the parents remembered that his six-year-old sister, out of her own terror, had told George that girls never needed that kind of operation.

The final piece of work related to George's pleasures in masturbation and his oedipally tinged conclusion that having boy feelings in his penis for his mother and sister would bring further medical trauma upon him. The parents themselves had been traumatized, first by having a damaged child and then by unsupported medical experiences. After the initial period of sharing, sorrow, and reliving of their panic and distress, they worked together with each other and the analyst very effectively in George's behalf. George responded within weeks. After six months of working via the parents, George was functioning in an age-appropriate masculine way at home and at school. He played with boys, loved fire trucks, never talked about wanting to be a girl, and still loved ballet.

The case was closed for the time being, with the parents understanding that the medical situation left George vulnerable to finding magical solutions at times of stress. They felt equipped to help him more effectively and also knew how well they could make use of professional assistance to enhance their parenting in good times and bad. They talked about coming back for help when George reached adolescence.

Parent Work on Behalf of Older Children

Working via the parent has traditionally been a method used mostly with parents of preschoolers, but we have found that the principles and techniques involved can sometimes usefully be applied across age groups.

Katrin's parents sought help because they felt their adopted fifteen-year-old daughter was in need of treatment, but she refused any suggestion to see someone, and her parents were afraid that pressure even to have an evaluation would make her run away from home. The analyst agreed to see the parents for a while to clarify their feelings about the situation and to see if it would be possible to find some ways to work with their daughter around the difficulties that were causing her to fail in school and disrupting her relationships with adults and peers.

In discussions with Katrin's parents, it became clear that they, particularly the mother, were overly involved in her body and daily care. Both parents were exceptionally anxious about Katrin and about aspects of the outside world—her mother would not drive on the freeway, and her father telephoned home to check on the family's safety several times daily. Many aspects of their own early histories were played out explicitly with their daughter. Issues of separation had become confused with their feelings about their late adoption of Katrin. They had been afraid that they would not be able to truly love her unless they "made her their own" by changing her name at the age of nearly two. Fear of feeling unconnected had led them to stay completely enmeshed in her psychological and practical life.

Over a period of eighteen months, Katrin's parents attended regular sessions to talk about their parenting. They were able to differentiate more from her, to sort out which were their feelings and which were Katrin's, and to begin to delimit areas of responsibility. Katrin's response to the changes in her parents was to grow considerably, giving up much of her rebellious behavior, while continuing to go her own way in pursuing an unconventional academic career.

Treatment via the parent for under-fives seems to work, among other reasons, because of the emotional availability of the young child and the parents' developmentally appropriate emotional closeness at that age. In Katrin's case, her parents' closeness to her represented a developmental arrest in their growth as parents, but provided a temporary entrée to the dynamics of their relationships. With insight into their overinvolvement, they returned to the path of progressive development as parents and were able to achieve appropriate separation from their daughter. When Katrin went on to professional training in another city, she was able to ask the analyst, whom she had never seen, for a referral for treatment in her own right.

Establishing the Need for the Child's Treatment

Once the parents and therapist have done as much as is possible in working via the parents, those areas of emotional pain, developmental arrest, and maladaptive behavior in the child that are internally generated and independent of current stressors may be discerned more clearly, and the need for individual therapy is evident to all concerned. A sense of shared conviction about the nature and seriousness of the problems and the strength of an established working relationship between parents and therapist give inestimable help to the therapeutic alliance if individual treatment of the child is undertaken. This underscores another critical factor: the analyst's conviction about the recommendation. Without this confidence we cannot work hard enough to find good explanations for our proposals, nor will we be able to sustain our commitment to the case through long and difficult times.

Confidence and conviction come more easily after years of experience, so how can a trainee convey such confidence to parents who are adaptively alert to any signs of inexperience, incompetence, insecurity, or uncertainty in applying unfamiliar techniques? The usual method is to keep the evaluation short and rely on parental anxiety and submission to authority to get a child's treatment started. We suggest that an extended evaluation can have a more genuinely beneficial outcome for the patient, the parents, and the trainee therapist or analyst.

A predoctoral intern was assigned her first child case, and during the third appointment, when she expected to give her recommendation to the parents, the mother asked, "Are you a student?" The student avoided answering the question directly, and her supervisor suggested that she call us to see what we might advise. The student had gathered good descriptions of the first-grader's difficulties, but little else was clear, so we said that we thought neither the therapist nor the parents were ready for a recommendation. We suggested that she tell the parents that she is indeed an advanced student and say that the mother was being a good, protective parent to ask. As a student, she brings her own knowledge and interest in child development as well as therapy, supervision, and consultation with senior child therapists, but mostly she will have the help of the parents, who know the most about their own child and are the most important people to that child. She could describe that the goal is to work together to figure out what the difficulties are about and what the parents can do themselves to help their boy. She will be working together with them for as long as it takes to get a clearer picture and see what works. If they eventually decide together that they have reached the limit of what parents can do with her support, then she will add individual work with the child while continuing to work with them.

The following week, the therapist told us that the meeting went very well. The parents liked the plan; felt respected; and appreciated her honesty, enthusiasm and willingness to consult others. They said that they had been feeling helpless, but now, as part of a team, they felt more hope that they would be able to work things out together.

The approach we feel most comfortable with is one of work with parents to help modify and shape the child's external world, which includes his or her parents' functioning and personalities. Work with the child will provide a private space for exploration and unfolding of the child's inner world. Through the lens of the therapeutic alliance we may see the complex necessity of establishing multiple alliances, balancing the needs of each. In work with children and adolescents there is an alliance with the child, with the parents, between the parents, and between the child and parents. The task of the therapist is to foster each of these; be alert to the obstacles, both practical and emotional, to these alliances; and provide help to tap into the positive forces in each party to maintain the alliances.

CHAPTER THREE

Initiating the Transformations of Evaluation

Although each situation is different, the following story of the evaluation phase with Henry and his parents can be used to illustrate the initiation of a sequence of transformations. Henry's parents began to shift from acute anxiety to realistic concern, then renewed denial, which, when confronted, required the transformation of guilt to concern. Finally, defensive withdrawal gave way to a renewal of primary parental love for the child. Only at that point was the alliance with Henry's parents sturdy enough for the child's own treatment to begin.

Four-year-old Henry's mother talked in the first phone conversation about his inability to separate from her and the degree of anxiety he seemed to experience at night. The parents were worried that these problems might interfere with his adjustment to school. In the first meeting, the parents' anxiety was acute. The mother felt sure that her son was severely disturbed and feared guiltily that she had damaged him. The father minimized Henry's problems, but also blamed his wife for any difficulties.

There was clearly long-standing friction between them about managing their son. They were united in their desire that the therapist provide a definite answer to their question about school adjustment. Like many parents, their conscious model of seeking help was that the therapist had the answer and would somehow generically know what was going on. Henry's parents presented one of the first transformative tasks, that of changing the authoritarian relationship model they carried into the meeting into a more collaborative one as a basis for an ongoing therapeutic alliance. The therapist had to find a way to begin to remodel their idea of the therapist's providing all answers so as to formulate together the questions the assessment should address.

The therapist agreed about the importance of their question, but suggested that the parents were the people who knew Henry best, and they could use both their knowledge and their feelings about him now and in the past to understand what was going on. The answers would emerge from pooling the knowledge from the parents, the therapist, and Henry. By examining all aspects of his development and functioning, joint questions could be formulated and the answers sought together in the assessment process. Thus the answers would be a shared achievement of the parents, Henry, and the analyst.

As the parents and therapist worked together to formulate the questions, many of the parents' fears and fantasies about Henry came to light. Henry's mother felt very close to her son; she had the sense that he was just like her and that she knew all the distress he was feeling. Yet his very dependence on her for all reality testing made her terrified that he might be psychotic. Her deep fear that she had damaged him in some basic way emerged in relation to this diagnostic question. Henry's father was ambivalent about his son's resemblance to himself as a child; the gratification to his vanity of Henry's identification was offset by memories of his own childhood unhappiness and miserable obsessionality. This material allowed the therapist to verbalize these parents' hurt and sorrow and their pain about Henry's difficulties. They could then begin to share these feelings with each other supportively, rather than deal with them by externalization and blame. This led to their increasing ability to see Henry's feelings as inside him, so starting the crucial transformation of perception of the difficulties from an external battle between parents and child to the internal conflicts with which Henry was struggling.

Understanding these worries of the parents not only brought out many additional symptoms and clarified the diagnostic assignment, but there was a further benefit in relation to the therapeutic alliance. The transformation of understanding Henry's problems as internal to him shifted the focus away from the parents and allowed them to imagine joining the therapist to understand together how to help Henry. The analyst could address directly the responsibility they did carry for some of Henry's problems and further proceed to help them appreciate their heeding Henry's signals of distress as an indication of their basic devotion to his needs and their own investment in being good parents. The lens of the therapeutic alliance tasks facilitated focus on the strengths these parents brought to the situation and a transformation in their perceptions of Henry's difficulties.

Henry's parents had been surprised by his evident relief and enthusiasm about the evaluation sessions. The analyst felt sure that Henry was not psychotic but indeed had many troubles. When this was conveyed to his parents, they first expressed their enormous relief, but then retreated quickly from discussion of Henry's ongoing anxieties. His father expressed continued annoyance over Henry's clinging; his mother seemed to withdraw her concern and sounded airily cynical about how "kids this age sure do seem to give their parents the runaround."

The analyst understood the parents' change in attitude as a defensive retreat from renewed feelings of helplessness and failure and wondered whether there might be a deeper unconscious wish to have him be severely disturbed, which was thwarted by the diagnosis. Because parents and analyst had been working together throughout the weeks of the evaluation, a relationship had been established that allowed for addressing the defense directly. The analyst took up the effective work the parents had done to recognize Henry's own worries as distinct from theirs and how this had already provided them and Henry with some relief. In the context of this shared experience of their positive parenting, direct questioning of their withdrawal was possible. Henry's mother then became curious about her change of attitude and wondered with the analyst whether Henry had triggered some deeper anxiety of her own.

A different set of problems arises when the therapist perceives serious difficulties in the parent's functioning, but the referral has been made for the child, and the parent does not recognize any problems of his or her own.

The Importance of Dual Goals of Treatment

Dual goals provide one solution to the technical problem of the parents' not being the designated patient. The work together that helped Henry's mother and father function more effectively as parents was also explicitly acknowledged as a goal of the evaluation and any eventual treatment. Henry's mother could see that the way they had worked with the analyst helped her child and made her feel like a better parent. So it was worth it to her in a new way to address some of her own issues. The parents and the analyst agreed to meet regularly once a week for a time to try to understand better what aspects of the parents' functioning might be affecting Henry adversely, particularly his father's anger and his mother's withdrawal.

Henry's father had earlier opened up the topic of his identification of Henry with himself as a child, and the analyst could wonder with him why he did this. Henry's mother, in describing some of Henry's mannerisms, realized that she was using words that better suited her older brother. He had been a deeply disturbed youngster who had terrorized her and her sister, but their parents and the extended family had all denied the problems until the boy became unmanageable in adolescence and was finally sent to a residential treatment center. As this history unfolded and mother became increasingly able to see the differences between Henry and her brother, Henry's father also saw that he was replaying a hostile, argumentative relationship with his younger brother whom he had always seen as demanding more of his mother's attention.

At this point, some major alliance tasks of the evaluation phase were accomplished, in that Henry's parents were seeing him much more as a separate individual, rather than as a transference object (for a full list of therapeutic alliance tasks in the evaluation phase, see table 2 in chapter 11). Traumatic guilt, from which they had recoiled, had been transformed into usable concern. They were anxious to have Henry enter his own treatment, and the analyst also continued to be concerned about Henry's ongoing distress and need for help. In the work with this family the recommendation followed naturally from the shared realization of Henry's own need for help.

As noted earlier, the evaluation phase has usually been given too little weight. In fact, the evaluation phase could be likened to the overture to an opera, an important section of the work in which all the themes are prefigured, however fleetingly. Transformation is an alliance task that is only begun in the evaluation and continues throughout each subsequent phase of treatment. But we need at least to hear strains of the various requisite transformations of parenting in the evaluation before we can confidently proceed to the body of the treatment.

The highly anxious single mother of eight-year-old Thea was referred to the child psychiatric clinic of the local hospital by both teachers and pediatricians because Thea was unable to concentrate. The psychiatric resident who saw them prescribed medication for the child and wanted to refer the mother for therapy, but the mother had made no mention of her own state, focusing the discussion solely on her child's troubles. So the resident recommended parent guidance with the idea that he would use this setting to provide therapy for the mother. This is a fairly common dilemma and solution that carries many pitfalls.

Thea's mother spent the year of the psychiatrist's rotation yelling at him, saying she herself did not need treatment, explaining that she would not be blamed for her child's problems, and calling at all hours to harangue the therapist for not helping her child more. The mother became known in the child clinic as "that angry mom," and none of the residents and interns the following year wanted to accept transfer of the case. A staff social worker took it on and sought consultation with one of us.

This seemed a situation where the options of referral to someone else for therapy of the parent or for parental therapy under the guise of parent guidance weren't viable. We suggested a third possibility—that the social worker suggest to the mother that they work together on how her parenting could support Thea as she grew and changed. The social worker could, in effect, start over with this mother, validating her positive wish to help Thea and enhancing her strengths for the child's sake. This alliance provided a holding environment for the mother in which she could use her ego strengths to support Thea's individual treatment. Thea was able to go off medication and showed significant improvement in school as well as improved friendships and interactions with her mother.

Thea's mother, reassured by her daughter's progress and mindful of her own role in promoting that growth, asked the social worker about how she could deal with her own problems that were less involved with Thea. Then the therapist could make a referral for the mother's individual therapy while assuring her that they would continue to work together on her parenting.

Thea's mother had been helped to marshal her strengths in the service of her daughter's needs. Through this process of work on her parenting function she rediscovered genuine internal resources for her own self-esteem, which in turn helped her better appreciate Thea.

The Need for Primary Parental Love

If we return to the case of Henry, we may see another way in which the element of love was brought into the situation. The analyst, who was also eager to begin work with Henry, was helped by remembering the framework of the various transformation tasks of the evaluation phase to hold off until another crucial element could be discerned. What was the theme not heard? It was the parents' pleasure in and with their child, a primary parental investment, akin to what we, drawing from Winnicott (1949), have called "objective love" (J. Novick and K. K. Novick 2000, 191). Without a note of this positive investment, their commitment to his treatment would not be strong enough to withstand the inevitable negative patches.

> The analyst and the parents were in accord about Henry's troubles, his anxieties and obsessional symptoms, but the analyst began to ask them about their perceptions of his strengths, his good qualities, what they enjoyed together with him and about him. Much struck, his mother burst into tears as she realized that it had been a long time since she and Henry had giggled together as they used to when reading his favorite Dr. Seuss books. His father had been so involved with Henry's fearfulness at the beach that he had forgotten the pleasure of long walks together to the ice cream store and his pride when Henry had been able to ride his bike with him in the park.

With the remembered and shared good feelings foreshadowing future pleasures, the analyst felt comfortable beginning treatment with Henry and continuing regular work with his parents. This was a situation where the technical structuring of the evaluation phase accomplished its aims, and the recommendation and beginning of treatment followed naturally from the transformative work. With the analyst using the techniques of working via the parent during an extended evaluation phase, Henry's parents could regain a sense of competence, transform their guilt into usable concern, and see their child as separate from themselves. As they began to separate their transferences to the child from his reality, they could see his own pain and regain their primary love for their son. These initial transformations, begun during the evaluation phase, continued throughout the treatment. Ongoing parent work allowed Henry to enter into and benefit from analysis and also enabled his parents to move through subphases of parenthood to consolidate their functioning in the adult developmental phase of parenthood.

CHAPTER FOUR

RECOMMENDATION, SETTING THE FRAME, AND WORKING CONDITIONS

Reactions to Recommendation for Treatment

As we move through the recommendation, the beginning phase of analysis, and the transition to the middle phase, the complex network of alliances—between the therapist and the child, between the therapist and the parents, between the parents, and between the parents and child—is further tested and strengthened. In the previous chapter we described the tasks and aims of the first part of the evaluation and saw how the initiation of various transformations strengthens the alliance with parents and helps them resume movement through the phase of parenthood. We noted that the recommendation for treatment can follow naturally from a relatively extended period of working with and through the parents, seeing what can be accomplished by that most conservative and economical method, but reaching the limits of that technique.

The transformations of the evaluation, however, are only just begun at that point, neither completely achieved nor consolidated. Often the actuality of the recommendation for treatment triggers an intense reaction in either or both of the parents, which may also reverberate for the analyst. Vulnerabilities in the parents' personalities can give rise to various anxieties and conflicts, revealing hitherto unseen dimensions of their personalities and presaging the difficult areas in the work ahead.

Exposure of Parental Pathology

One potential pitfall is that parenting can be a hidden, denied, and frequent outlet for perverse sadomasochistic functioning in adults (J. Novick and K. K. Novick 1996b; K. K. Novick 1997). A major mechanism in sadomasochistic pathology is externalization, a defense aimed at avoiding narcissistic pain consequent on accepting devalued aspects of the self. Children are available, helpless targets for maternal and paternal externalizations. This lays the groundwork for a sadomasochistic relationship with the child. Children who are the objects of parental externalizations show severe disturbance with mental pain and conflict rooted in the acceptance of a devalued or idealized self. They are unable to integrate real, positive aspects of themselves with the conscious self-representation (J. Novick and Kelly 1970), and they see themselves alternatively as victims and bullies in sadomasochistic interactions with their parents. This sets the stage for the development of similar pathological mechanisms in the child, thus creating the transgenerational effect of sadomasochistic functioning. Working on parenting brings this cycle into the open.

When we set about examining parenting issues during the evaluation of a child, we risk confronting defensive efforts to maintain intact a source of gratification and needed narcissistic equilibrium. A long-enough evaluation can at least give the analyst a sense of what lies ahead in treatment and some warning of potential sources of intense reactions to a recommendation for treatment for the child. The frequent experience of unexpected treatment refusal is often due to the analyst's depriving him- or herself of this critical information.

Crediting Parents' Wish to Do a Good Job

At the same time, the wish to be a better parent is often the only or best entrée to motivation for change in adults. The efforts of the analyst to generate a therapeutic alliance provide a framework that may allow parents access to their best selves in the context of the child's treatment. It is crucial that hope and positive feelings in the parents be fostered and maintained. The therapist helps parents regain their primary parental love for the child and find something to genuinely respect and admire in the child.

But analysts also need a source of hope and conviction to sustain them, and this is best found through contact sustained long enough to discover what is admirable in the parents. As we noted earlier, seeking help is usually a sign that parents have entered into the phase of psychological parenthood and are willing to suffer something for the sake of their child's needs. Therapists can build on this positive fact and credit parents with the wish to be the best parents they can be.

Therapists need to feel at least a glimmering of this initial respect, since child work can bring us into contact with severe adult disturbances. Parents of child patients are often much more troubled than adult patients who seek help in their own right. For instance, Henry's parents were each very disturbed. His father was a lifelong obsessional neurotic with gaps in his conscience, superego lacunae that led him to flout the law habitually in front of his children. His feelings were inaccessible except for unpredictable moments of overwhelming rage, and his characteristic tone with his wife and children was demeaning. Henry's mother suffered from psychosomatic symptoms, debilitating fears, and a hysterical need for perfection in her surroundings, her person, and the children. Always on the coffee table in the all-white living room of the family home was a photo album that contained gory pictures of Henry's birth.

Also not detailed in our focus on the parent work during Henry's evaluation was his extensive symptomatology and nascent character pathology. Henry's self-representation was not of a human boy, but of a part robot with omnipotent powers. His multiple tics, obsessions, and phobias, coupled with the mechanical quality of his functioning and his lack of visible affect, made diagnoses of borderline condition or Asperger's syndrome plausible. Thus he was a very difficult prospect for analysis, and his parents' pathology threatened their relationship with him and potentially with the therapist. Without the framework of the therapeutic alliance tasks in the work with Henry's parents, the pressure of the parents' transference might have made the parent work degenerate into the kind of sadomasochistic interaction typical of each grouping in the family. Therefore, in order to counteract this possibility in the initial parent work, we emphasize the positive qualities and strengths parents and children bring. This provides a bridge to open-system functioning and the possibility of choosing an alternative way to relate to the child.

Parental Anxieties

With each parental anxiety, at any point in treatment, there may be a corresponding issue for the analyst (for a summary listing of parental anxieties, defenses, resistances, and therapeutic responses, see table 2 in chapter 11).

Alienation of Affection—Kidnapping the Child—Negative Therapeutic Motivation

A major parental anxiety is that the child's affections or loyalties will be stolen by the analyst (E. Furman 1997). Guilty and defensive, out of touch with their love for their child, parents come to the situation feeling, consciously or unconsciously, that they may deserve to have their child taken away. To the extent that they are angry and frustrated with the child's lack of response to their efforts to ameliorate the situation, they may also wish to hand the child over, dump the child on the therapist, and get rid of the trouble and pain the child's difficulties have caused. This wish can cause further guilt that may be defended against by clinging to the child and undermining the development of his new relationship with the therapist. In extreme cases, this is one of the determinants of a negative therapeutic motivation, in which child and mother unconsciously combine to make the treatment fail (J. Novick 1980).

The following case, treated many years ago, illustrates collusion between parents and child that seeks to undermine and destroy the treatment almost before it gets started. At that time, without a conceptual framework to structure interventions with the parents, and in the presence of severe pathology in the mother and borderline functioning with passivity in the father, the analyst began a treatment of the child before establishing necessary transformations or a baseline of a working relationship with the parents. Despite the fact that the parents ostensibly agreed to the recommendation for analysis, the treatment was not fully established.

Charlie, fifteen, had been in analysis from the age of eleven. Originally he had been referred to his first analyst for uncontrolled rages and attacks on his younger brother. He and his parents saw the first period of work as a waste of time. He had spent each session reading comics, slowly sipping from a container of soda pop, and talking to his mother by calling her on the telephone. His first analyst moved away, and he was transferred to a second analyst. When first seen, Charlie looked more like a schoolchild than an adolescent about to turn sixteen. He was failing in every area of functioning. He had gone through a progressive school without learning anything and would likely be unable to graduate from high school. He had no friends, was bullied and teased, and showed severe disturbances in all areas of internal functioning. In the sessions he shouted that analysis was a prison, that everything would be fine if he didn't have to be there, and that he wanted his mother to be his therapist. After each session Charlie used the pay phone to call his mother and tell her what had been discussed.

Charlie knew that he had made the earlier analysis fail and was aware that he wanted to do it again. During this time, his parents were very supportive and insisted that he attend treatment. They assiduously kept the analyst informed of all the "terrible things" Charlie said about his therapy and offered sympathy to the analyst for Charlie's contempt and his failure to change.

Gradually, however, as Charlie began to develop a positive transference and the beginning of a therapeutic alliance, he began to change. As each change became apparent or was about to be translated into action, however, Charlie's mother would do something to obliterate both his and the analyst's roles, so that the credit for the positive change would become hers alone. Charlie's need to stay a little boy both mentally and physically, which had eventuated in a delayed puberty, began to yield to concentrated work in the treatment. Charlie began to grow and mature. As soon as these developments began to show, the mother took him to a "growth clinic" where he was given hormone injections. Charlie became physically mature and grew to average height, but he did not attribute any of these changes to something internal, linked to the analytic work. He saw the physical changes as entirely due to his mother's intervention. Each further progressive move was similarly taken over by his mother, from his leaving school and starting a job to his first sexual experience. Thus each success became a source of failure and humiliation—the analyst's failure and his—and Charlie remained tied to an image of an omnipotent mother as the only one who could grant all his wishes. (Adapted from J. Novick and K. K. Novick 1996b, 276–77)

What could not be accomplished at the beginning of Charlie's case were parental shifts from external causes to internal conflicts, nor could his mother see him as an individual separate from her use of him as a repository of externalizations that she needed to maintain her own tenuous self-esteem. She was unable to join in the goal of changing the character of her relationship to one of respect, love, mutuality, and shared progressive development, to what we have also called an open-system relationship.

Parents' Own Therapy

As we noted in chapter 1, analysts have traditionally hoped to deal with parental pathology by referring parents to their own treatment. Cases like that of Charlie have convinced us that work with parents by the child's analyst throughout all phases of treatment is necessary to address the dual goals of the child work. Charlie's mother had her own therapist and the availability of a child guidance worker, but the situation needed focused attention on the dynamics of her parenting function and the nature of the parent-child relationship if there was to be any hope of lasting change in the family. The details of her interaction with Charlie were not part of her own treatment, and the time needed to work on issues there left Charlie behind.

Parental Guilt as an Interference

During the evaluation we establish explicitly with parents that one of the treatment goals is restoring their relationship with the child. A tone of respect for their knowledge, perceptions, good intentions, and renewed love toward their child, coupled with genuine collaboration in the process of coming to an understanding of the child's troubles, may provide enough counterbalance to crushing guilt and anxiety for parents to tolerate their child's important independent relationship with the analyst. Attention must, however, be paid to this dimension throughout treatment.

"Will My Child Be Labeled?"

Another concern frequently expressed by parents is fear of stigmatization of their child. Parental worries about their child being ostracized or teased come from many levels, but almost always represent issues that are more the parents' than the child's. One root is the intense shame parents feel at exposing what they experience as their failure to be good parents by entering into an assessment and treatment situation. Defensive externalization onto the child as the potential humiliated victim is one way to deal with shame. A more complex dynamic sometimes appears when a parent sets up this fear in order to feel capable and protective, that is, to regain a sense of parental competence. Exploration with the parents about the reactions they have had from family members often elicits conscious material that can be linked to earlier discussions about guilt and responsibility and opens up an avenue of ongoing work. Anxiety about other children's teasing can sometimes be countered with the analyst's knowledge of children's reactions to each other. We have many, many experiences to recount of the kindness, empathy, curiosity, and occasional envy that classmates show to children in treatment. Adolescents often bring their friends to sessions, wanting perhaps to put together their good feelings for their therapist and their other important relationships. Pointing this out, with the gentle suggestion that this is more of a worry for parents than for children, can help parents take their externalization back in and work with it.

Fear of Feelings

Many parents worry that treatment will be "too much" for their child. When we inquire about this idea, fears and fantasies emerge from many levels. The very elements that have led to denial and symptom formation in the family are called into play with this anxiety. The pathological belief, often shared by child and parents, that feelings are dangerously powerful, begins to emerge. The anxiety that the child will break down offers an opportunity to describe for parents in more detail exactly what will happen in treatment and how it is designed to help the child work at a manageable pace. We talk about building the relationship gradually with the child, being with him as he plays, talks, and begins to let the analyst into his world. Over time the analyst becomes an important companion with whom the child can notice how he experiences things, manages his feelings, and interacts with others. We tell the parents that, within the safety of the relationship, which also affords a lot of pleasure, alternatives and the interferences with them can be canvassed, allowing the child the possibility of growth and change.

Eight-year-old Joseph's parents brought him for an evaluation because of his stormy tantrums when frustrated and his trouble trying to do

49

schoolwork in the face of a dysgraphic learning disability. His teacher was violently opposed to therapy, as she felt that Joseph was already too "stressed." His parents, despite their deep sadness at Joseph's predicament, wished that they could solve his problems by simply relieving him of anything demanding in his life. They too feared that treatment would compound, rather than ameliorate, Joseph's difficulties. They accepted a treatment plan to begin with two sessions a week as a preparatory phase to intensive work, with the idea that this might reassure them about Joseph's capacity to tolerate the work of therapy. As they saw his increasing relaxation and resiliency, they were able to accept the recommendation for analysis.

Practical Problems as Real and as Resistance

Another type of parental resistance emerges in relation to practical arrangements. Parents are understandably concerned about the burden that intensive treatment for one child places on their daily family life, their finances, and often on siblings. First of all, the reality must be acknowledged. We do this verbally and by making every effort to design a schedule that is mutually convenient and feasible. We also try to make sure that parents are not contracting for something that will turn out to be unmanageable—resentment and fatigue will scuttle the treatment when it has barely begun. For instance, it will probably rarely work to have younger siblings spend every session in the waiting room.

When Will Treatment End? Termination Starts at the Very Beginning

We have found that it is only possible to address the deeper levels when practical realities have been dealt with. Then we may begin to look with parents at their fears that treatment will go on forever. With this access we begin to generate termination criteria. Rather than constricting the work by giving parents a specific time estimate, which may rapidly become their unilateral treatment plan, we describe restoration to progressive development as the goal. This will be seen in the child's acceleration of forward development, in a renewed pleasure in his own functioning and in the parent-child relationship. This is an accessible and logical development from earlier discussions of symptoms and anxieties as interferences to progressive development. With these termination criteria in mind, parents and analyst are set to work together to monitor areas where progress has resumed and those where there is still little movement.

Inclusion of these termination criteria from the very beginning is a further application of the concept of two systems of self-esteem regulation. Establishing the description of progressive development in terms of growth in open-system functioning allows us to note with parents the contrast when closed-system functioning persists or reappears. Continuation and maintenance of the treatment then make sense to parents.

Transforming Guilt into Usable Concern

A long evaluation and period of working with the parents may also seem to have drawbacks. The referral is usually made at a point of crisis. If the parents have organized their own feelings and personalities around externalization of failure and badness onto the child, a prolonged evaluation may constitute a threat to parents' defensive position. In order to protect themselves, parents may resist the gradual approach we are advocating and quickly seek help elsewhere. It could be argued that to delay individual treatment of the child is to lose the window of opportunity provided by parental anxiety and helplessness.

Parental anxiety is indeed a powerful motivator that fuels most initial contacts with a therapist. We suggest, however, that one task of the evaluation is to transform guilty anxiety into constructive concern. Several assumptions are implicit in this idea. In the evaluation, and over time during extended work with parents before taking a child into treatment, we are also eliciting and fostering primary parental love, which is only possible when the child is seen as a separate, valued person in his or her own right. In addition, we are assessing the degree of sadomasochistic enmeshment between parent and child, which denies autonomy and ties them together through externalizations. Parent work can often successfully dissipate initial parental anxiety and bring real improvement in the situation. Despite the therapist's feeling that the child still needs individual treatment, many parents feel relieved and want to stop at that point in the extended evaluation, refusing the recommendation for individual therapy or analysis. Some analysts try to invoke professional authority to pressure parents; others back down and may thereby collude with parental denial. We build upon the extended parent work to address these issues in a different way.

Joe was a defiant ten-year-old who lied habitually and was dangerously aggressive with his younger sister. He had started bullying other children at school; his teachers had insisted on the referral. The analyst worked with Joe's parents over several months on their inability to set limits, their repetition of their own abusive histories as they allowed Joe to abuse them, and their use of Joe in their marital struggles. After six months of parent work, Joe could manage his anger, was doing better at school, and was much more cooperative with his parents. It had been crucially important to help the father be more present in the family and more active with Joe.

At this point the parents expressed their pleasure in the progress and suggested that they see the analyst occasionally for parent guidance, but backed away from the idea that Joe needed any help on his own. In their relief at his changed behavior, they had not noticed that he had become a sad, lonely, withdrawn boy who seemed to lack zest or pleasure and pride in his achievements. He spent most of his time in his room playing computer games. When the analyst expressed his concern and wondered if this represented a self-punitive trend, the parents said they had noticed Joe's new "morbid" interest in death.

At this point the analyst could emphasize the importance of an individual treatment to help Joe find a better solution to his conflicts. The analyst described what the sequence sounded like to him: the effect of the parent work had been to help Joe internalize some responsibility for his actions. But he had done this in the service of maintaining the idea that he was magically and powerfully responsible for his sister and parents and could only protect them from his anger by withdrawing. The mother then asked what would happen to this dynamic in adolescence, and she associated to her own teenage suicide attempt. At that point, when Joe's functioning made emotional sense to the parents, they accepted the recommendation of analysis. Rather than focusing predominantly on Joe's behavior, they were able to think about his experience of himself as a whole person and offer their son a chance to build alternative internal solutions.

Confidentiality and the Hierarchy of Treatment Values

Perhaps the major objection raised by many therapists to working with the parents of their child or adolescent patients is the issue of confidentiality. Therapists worry about the child's security of communication and relationship and about losing the child's trust. How can one assure the child of the safety and inviolability of the child's therapeutic space? Can the therapist rely upon her own discretion to protect the child's privacy? Analysts have traditionally solved this problem by avoidance of parent work. One source of the difficulty is restricting the definition of treatment goals to the child alone. When we suggest dual goals for any treatment— that is, when we include restoration of the parent-child relationship and growth in parental development in our shared aims—the legitimate field of the work is expanded. Nevertheless, the issue is genuine. We know that we have to devise techniques that protect the child's privacy, that help parents tolerate the frustration of not knowing everything, that foster greater communication and sharing between parents and child, and that redefine separateness and autonomy between them.

As we have worked to understand our experience in treating families, we have realized that there is a hierarchy of clinical values that we apply to treatments of patients of all ages. The establishment of safety— for the patient, the parents, and the therapist—is paramount. It is in the best interests of the child that he or she be kept safe from harm. These are the priorities of the therapeutic setting for the therapist. Trust and security are crucial ingredients of the sense of safety; knowing that thoughts and feelings will be respected as belonging to one's private mental life allows for gradual relaxation into sharing them with the analyst. Progress along the developmental line of the sense of self includes increasing reliance on the privacy of one's mind. Knowing that dangerous actions toward others or the self will be addressed definitively also provides a sense of security to the child who fears his own loss of control; he then feels that his impulses will be checked with the help of another.

The work of the evaluation begins to establish the idea that the child is a separate person with his own mental life. It is a small logical step to the concept of the privacy of the child's material, but a very difficult one for parents. They have been used to knowing everything that their child does and have thought that they know everything he thinks. Not knowing is a real deprivation that gives rise to parental worries and creates a space for dire fantasies. Parents also fear the secret hostility of the child's communications. They worry about the revelation of secrets and that they may be exposed as failures. Similarly the child may feel torn by loyalty conflicts when talking about home or parents.

CHAPTER FOUR

The Distinction between Privacy and Secrecy

As noted above, a major worry for therapists contemplating work with parents is that it would actually, or would seem to the child to, violate confidentiality. Many go further in thinking that work with parents runs counter to the adolescent developmental task of separation. Parental intrusion and inability to separate can be seen as the major obstacles to adolescent treatment and growth. Many analysts who work with adolescents therefore regularly refer parents to another clinician for ancillary work. Our view of adolescence sees the major developmental tasks for both parents and children as involving transformation of the self and the relationship, rather than separation, particularly physical separation. Therefore, as we will discuss at greater length in the chapter on middle phase work, we think the adolescent's analyst should be responsible for protecting the privacy of the patient while supporting improved communication between parents and child and analyzing interferences to free exchange.

We talk with parents from the beginning about the difference between privacy and secrecy. Privacy is a given of mental life and a right related to mutual respect between separate individuals. Secrecy is motivated withholding that carries a connotation of knowledge used to feel powerful in relation to excluded others. It often arises when intrusion and control are issues in the parent-child relationship. Intimations of these conflictual dimensions emerge during the evaluation and give the analyst warning of potential separation and boundary problems. Differentiating between privacy and secrecy gives the therapist a needed vocabulary to explore family secrets, parents' secrets, and the child's secrets.

Exclusion and Loss Contrasted with Autonomy and Transformation

We address parental feelings of exclusion by reminding them of the treatment goal of greater closeness with their children. It is another chance to introduce the concept that development does not mean their child just grows away from them. Rather, it means that they and their child create new ways to be close at the new level. This is particularly important in relation to adolescents. Our model of normality and pathology assumes that the goal of each developmental phase is transformation. Therefore we do not see adolescence as a time of separation, particularly not necessarily physical separation (DeVito, Novick, and Novick 1994). Transformation of the relationship to the self, others, and reality is the major task of adolescent development.

We assure the parents that we will use our regular meetings together not only to follow what is happening at home and in their parenting, but also to keep them in general touch with progress in their child's treatment. We point out that the inner drama is similar for us all—the scenarios are of love, death, birth, creativity, frustration, jealousy, wishes, rivalries, mastery, and so forth. The child's own version of the story is private; the details belong to him. We will include as much as possible without interfering with the child's need for privacy, safety, and space.

Eight-year-old Ned was used to deflecting his parents' attention from his minor infractions by precocious intellectual joking or playing the clown. His parents were generally very permissive, but felt strongly about bad language and sexually tinged behavior. Ned initially found it hard to believe when his analyst described therapy as an "unusual place where you can say anything you want to, kind of like the whole room is your own mind, so your private thoughts and feelings are safe here. When we do things, we have to keep you and me and the room safe—actions are different—and that will help keep it feeling safe for the thoughts." Ned pondered this for a minute, looked quizzical, then said, "Shit." When the analyst said nothing, Ned grinned.

Later in his treatment, when Ned reported sex play with a slightly older boy, the analyst could work with him in sessions about his excitement, shame, and guilt, but also discuss his conflicts over telling his parents what was going on. The analyst said to Ned that he needed his parents' help to deal with his entanglement with the older boy and that the analyst would help him talk to his parents about this. At the same time, the analyst worked with Ned's parents on their reactions to his ordinary sexual curiosity and helped them develop more comfortable criteria for judging when Ned's excitement was excessive. This allowed for talking about the need for them to support Ned's development of good judgment about activities with other boys by closer monitoring and discussion with their son. Without an explicit report from the analyst, the parents took note of Ned's changed affect in relation to the neighbor boy, gently questioned Ned, and were able to talk with him constructively about limiting time alone with the other child.

Family Secrets

The destructive impact of family secrets on children's psychological development and functioning is well established. They can have a similarly undermining effect on a treatment, producing confusion and lack of genuine emotional contact, negatively affecting the formation and maintenance of the therapeutic alliance. Sometimes parents and therapists work well together for a time and then agree on the shared observations that lead to a recommendation for individual treatment for the child or adolescent, but parents still balk at the actual commitment.

Therapists are understandably frustrated and confused at such times—the anxieties we have described above have at least been broached and many resistances addressed, yet something stops the parents. At this point parents may suddenly come up with various alternatives, such as medication, boarding school, different visitation schedules in divorced families, and any number of short-term interventions. Since we have begun to develop our model of working with parents, this problem has come up less frequently for us and for our students. Nevertheless, such cases do still occur; increasingly we have wondered if such seemingly deep resistance relates to a parental fear that the child in treatment will reveal some dark, shameful real or imagined secret. This emerged in a case evaluated over an extended period by one of our students.

> When the parents of ten-year-old Louise refused individual treatment, the therapist remarked to them that she was puzzled, as they had worked well together and had seemed to agree on the child's continuing need. Was there, she asked, some family issue or secret that had not been mentioned that they were concerned would come out in the child's treatment? The mother blushed, and the father angrily told the therapist that she was "out of line." The meeting soon ended, with the parents refusing to make another appointment. A few weeks later, the mother wrote to the therapist saying that there was something problematic going on in the family and that she hoped someday to be able to talk further about treatment for the child.
>
> Six months later the mother contacted the therapist wanting treatment for her daughter. At the first meeting, the mother told the therapist that she and father had separated. They were in the process of obtaining a divorce. The secret she had been unable to reveal was her ex-

husband's alcoholism that had led to his abusing her and the children physically when he was drunk.

The analyst first did some further work with the mother around the loyalty to father that she and Louise had demonstrated during the first evaluation. The therapist acknowledged how hard their situation had been and how much everyone in the family must need help sorting out the difficult feelings. Stressing the importance of candor in potential treatment, the therapist helped the mother see the importance of talking with Louise about what they had experienced and worked on how to do this, as well as how to tell the child that the therapist knew about the troubles in their background. When treatment began, Louise did not avoid or deny the issue of parental discord or her father's physical abuse. She was able to talk about her love for her father but also about her fear and confusion.

An analyst has a difficult choice to make in a situation such as that with Louise's parents. One can decide that it is impossible to address and back down gracefully, unless the parents unilaterally preempt that decision, as Louise's initially did. Even then we try to leave the door open for the future. A surprising number of parents return, often many years later.

Another possibility is to take a more oblique approach, using the discussion of common worries about treatment to raise the idea that many children worry about the therapist reading their minds; that is, they fear a loss of control over what they tell the therapist and what the therapist will find out. In such a description, we include that parents can share this worry, as almost every family has memories of upsetting or difficult situations. We note that a goal of treatment is to make thoughts and feelings manageable, to master what seems overwhelming, and to enhance communication in the family. But we also describe the gradual pace of the work and stress the inherent privacy of the setting. Such reassurance is sometimes adequate for parents to allow treatment to begin and for therapists to feel enough security that they will eventually be able to address whatever the troubling secret may be.

Sometimes the therapist forms the impression that there is a secret when the actuality is that a major event or issue is being unconsciously denied by all family members. This was the case, for example, through the evaluation and beginning of treatment with eleven-year-old Johnny, who was referred for anxiety and learning difficulties. Treatment began on the basis of generally good beginning transformations with parents, but the therapist continued to feel that something was being omitted. Because of the good alliance begun during the long evaluation, the therapist could directly ask the parents whether there was something important that was going unsaid. The parents were puzzled at first, but then associated to the therapist's use of the word "missing." They realized that they had never talked about Johnny's having an undescended testicle. In this instance the therapist had responded to the unconscious use of a defense, rather than a conscious parental protection of a family secret.

When the Child Has a Secret

Young children sometimes bring guilty worries to evaluation sessions, relieved to be able to tell someone what has been preying on their minds. This is significant material that the analyst can talk with the child about as something to work on over time—eventually the child will be able to share this with his parents if it still feels important.

Adolescents' secrets are often more dangerous, including accounts of thoughts, fantasies, impulses, and actions. We are very explicit with adolescents and with their parents that thoughts are private, actions are public. When teenagers do something that endangers themselves or others, it does not fall under the mantle of confidentiality, but is something that we will discuss with the patient in terms of how to talk with their parents or some other adult about the situation. Self-injurious activities, risk-taking behavior, and suicidal gestures and actions are all possible candidates for joint disclosure to parents or other authorities. This calls for fine judgments on the part of the therapist and is one of the areas of greatest stress during treatment of young people. But setting the conditions explicitly at the beginning reassures analyst, parents, and usually the adolescent patient that the therapist will be realistic and do his best to keep the situation safe and secure.

When Parents Have a Secret

A lengthy evaluation gives therapists opportunities to pick up intimations of family secrets—almost all families have some events or family members or actions that they are reluctant to talk about. There is a whole spectrum of reasons for such material to be omitted during even a long evaluation, with a corresponding range of feelings in the therapist around such gaps. Secrets can play an important role throughout treatment. At the time of setting the working conditions, there are three typical scenarios.

One is when the therapist has a distinct and uneasy feeling that something is being suppressed consciously. This can be a time bomb for a treatment, but, as we noted above, describing the universality of the situation to parents and making an explicit reminder of the value of candor are ways to invite parents to be more forthcoming. Describing straightforwardness as a necessary dimension of the collaborative relationship of parent work can be included in the list of working conditions. Another crucial issue can be addressed in the context of family secrets. The reason that the therapist plans to work so hard to help parents make good judgments about how, when, and whether to share information with their child is that the analyst is not trying to usurp the parents' position. Rather than being only a dreadful pitfall and interference to therapy, the existence of family secrets can also be used to stress the primacy of the parent-child relationship and reassure parents that they are the most important people in their children's lives.

A second is a vague sense that something is missing, without the analyst feeling the annoyance inherent in being strung along or excluded. As we described above in terms of the operation of a defense, this may be a signal that parents have either truly repressed something significant or that they are genuinely unaware that an element of family history matters in the etiology of their child's troubles. The solution in this case is to continue working, tolerating the frustration that not all data can be collected before starting treatment.

Third, and most demanding, is the situation when parents disclose something to the therapist, but enjoin silence: "we don't want our child to know about this." This is a very difficult situation for the therapist, who has several important judgments to make. She must decide whether it is possible to withhold the knowledge from the child—is it possible to work honestly with a child if one knows, for instance, that the child is adopted, but the child doesn't? She may feel she must decide, or advise the parents, as to whether the information should be kept from the child—is it helpful or harmful to a child to know that a parent has had an affair? She must decide what her role is in relation to bringing reality to the child.

All of these situations share the characteristic that they provide opportunities to help parents understand how treatment is going to work. In each instance, the therapist can use the dual goals of treatment to help steer a course. Keeping in mind that improved parent-child communication is part of improved parent-child relationships and that the nature of the desired relationship is one of an open and loving partnership according to the needs and capacities of all parties, the analyst can stress to the parents that they will be working together to define how to make judgments about what to share with the child, how, and when.

Loyalty Conflicts for Therapists—Feeling Caught between Two Parties

Therapists' concerns about difficulties in handling confidentiality when parents are seen regularly can also be due to our own discomfort at being put in a position of feeling caught between two parties. Loyalty conflicts and internal tensions are hard to bear; they can even interfere with our capacity to listen to the patient. These are important signals of child or parental externalization onto the analyst of impulses, feelings, or ego functions. Sooner or later these defensive externalizations will have to be addressed in treatment and in the parent work.

This can be especially true when working with divorcing or divorced parents. In the course of this book there are numerous clinical examples of such work and the strain it puts on all parties. The prevalence of divorce, the disproportionate number of children of divorced parents needing therapeutic help, and the fact that many therapists are themselves divorced may blunt us to the actuality of divorce as a major disruption that often reaches the level of traumatic overwhelming. Some divorced parents claim that they have moved on and harbor no ill feelings toward each other. We have never found this to be the whole story; at some point in the work, the therapist and the child patient are inevitably drawn into a continuing sadomasochistic battle between the parents. There are many different forms this can take; with Linda, described below, there was a complex background of externalizations intermingled with the history of her parents' marriage.

> Linda was the nine-year-old daughter of two professional parents who had each been in analysis and claimed that their divorce had been amicable, with no residual hard feelings. The mother, however, seemed espe-

cially hard on Linda, frequently becoming flooded with rage at her little girl. Linda too was a very angry child and was well practiced in knowing exactly what would most provoke her mother. In parent work with the mother, the initial focus was on better ways to avoid being provoked, but there was clearly something in the intensity and frequency of the mother's anger that spoke to the presence of more complex dynamics.

The therapist and mother began to track what in particular she found so infuriating in Linda. One day the mother said, "It's obvious—right there in front of my face. I get furious when she acts like her father. I hated him for those characteristics, and now I hate her for the same reasons. What can I do? I can't divorce her!" In the subsequent work, they could unravel the source of her anger as stemming from externalization of hated parts of herself onto her husband. Now with him out of the picture she was repeating that dynamic with her daughter.

In this instance we can see that hurt and rage between the partners in a problematic marriage can end with divorce but can continue to be played out with the children of divorced parents.

When the Evaluation Can Be Short

There are circumstances when it quickly becomes clear that the parents have indeed tried many constructive approaches before seeking formal help. They have struggled through many of the transformations, are responsive, and are relatively ready to begin working with the analyst in the service of the child's treatment. Then individual treatment can begin after a short period of time. Careful assessment of the nature of the parents' anxiety is needed in order to differentiate between these constructive situations and those where, as with Charlie's family, the push for treatment masks parents' use of the child and the therapist for their own emotional needs.

Indicators for an Extended Evaluation

A hallmark of urgency that means later trouble is a sense of parental demandingness that makes the therapist feel backed into a corner. Signals to be alert for might include the therapist volunteering for heroic scheduling or failing to communicate standard information, for instance, about payment. Parental demands may be coupled with a flattering idealization of the analyst that threatens to seduce the analyst into compliance before properly addressing the alliance tasks of the evaluation. This can alternatively take the form of heroic compliance on the part of parents with the therapist's schedule or arrangements. This was the situation in a case supervised many years ago:

> At the insistence of their doctor, the parents brought their sixteen-year-old son Bill for treatment due to his severe psychogenic chest pains and fears of death. The parents were seen as forthcoming and cooperative during the standard short evaluation, as was Bill in his interviews. In addition to his anxiety, Bill was also failing at school; was increasingly aggressive and abusive to others, especially girls; and was engaged in numerous delinquent behaviors. Treatment began forthwith, and the parents expressed extravagant relief.
>
> Bill came to his first session with his shirt unbuttoned down to the waist and lolled suggestively in his chair, seeming to expect a sexual response from his female therapist. He saw no difficulties with the times or frequencies of sessions and seemed to expect to stay all day, every day. By the end of the first session he said he was bored and, by the end of the second, announced that everything had changed and he felt much better. During the third session he presented what turned out be his mother's explanation for all his problems. He blamed his principal and all his teachers for failing to capture his interest at school. His mother then convinced the school to give him a special program and hired her own sister to tutor Bill. Everyone felt better.
>
> Bill did not come to his fourth session, and his mother telephoned, telling the therapist, "You must be so disappointed." The therapist admitted to puzzlement and concern and arranged with the parents for them to attend weekly sessions, which they did for the next four months. During these meetings the mother spoke of herself as the only one who had ever been able to respond to Bill's needs. He had been a difficult child from birth, but she could handle him. The referral had come during a period when she felt helpless to meet his needs, including his increasing anger. Although she made no conscious connection with her feelings of inadequacy, she described this same period as one in which Bill first began to make his sexual wishes more apparent at home, as he had done with the therapist in the first session.

In analytic work with adolescents, we have seen a number of cases where patients insisted that their parents had a claim on them sexually, that their sexual wishes, usually passive ones, belonged to their mothers. Their parents often feel that they are failures as parents if they cannot gratify the child's sexual impulses. Unable to do so, and unwilling to allow anyone else the possibility, they encourage regression to modes of functioning like the power struggles of toddlerhood, which they can participate in and gratify.

In the parent sessions it emerged that Bill's mother had suffered a serious gynecological condition, eventuating in surgery, just before the referral. In the months prior to the operation, she had not been able to have intercourse, and she had been frigid from anxiety afterward. Her motivation for continuing to meet with Bill's analyst was her conscious concern about her sexual inhibition and her feelings of sexual failure. Her material revealed clearly that she felt she was failing her child. She feared his rage, felt that it confirmed her failure, and felt doomed to death and abandonment. When the analyst noted how important these feelings were in understanding Bill's difficulties, the mother walked out in the middle of the session. She telephoned the next day to accuse the therapist of thinking she was a failure, then turned it around to accuse the therapist of failing to fix the situation. She never returned, and neither did Bill. This mother had managed to shift her externalizations of failure onto the analyst and could then renew her pathological tie with Bill. (Adapted from J. Novick and K. K. Novick 1996b, 272–75)

In retrospect, the parents' seamless pressure for immediate treatment was a danger signal. The ease of making arrangements was unrealistic, with a magical aura that everything and anything was possible. This is in contrast to the reality of most people's lives, where work and school schedules and other obligations all have to be juggled and adjusted to fit treatment in. Both the parents and Bill were looking for simple solutions, rather than seeming ready to engage in work that would be arduous at times. Parents who are truly ready to move quickly through an evaluation usually do not demand or expect instant action. They are often willing to explore a little further and welcome the opportunity to understand more.

Further Reasons to Complete Evaluation before Beginning Therapy

The recommendation, setting the frame, and discussing the working arrangements are part of the end of the evaluation phase. We have found that there is a series of issues that is often elided, dismissed as merely business related and not as important as the emotional/psychological issues that represent the content of the work. Our experience has been that relegating the business, or "nuts and bolts," to a lesser position generally serves defensive needs. If these administrative issues are not realistically addressed in a way that is consistent with forging an open and collaborative therapeutic alliance with parents, the treatment may eventually founder. In line with the idea of a collaborative relationship and open-system rootedness in reality, we give parents very clear statements of our working arrangements at the stage of making the recommendation for treatment. There is a chance to talk these through at the outset so that no one is surprised. Each analyst develops his or her own practices, but we have found that it establishes a baseline against which resistances may be measured if we start with explicit guidelines. Most important is that an extended evaluation establishes the idea that everything has meaning; then our working arrangements are not seen only as idiosyncratic whims, but as ways of conveying and establishing the importance of the treatment to all parties. We discuss fees, billing practices, responsibility for missed sessions, illnesses, vacations, rescheduling, modes of communication, and so forth. We ask for payment to be made at a regular time each month.

Thirty Days' Notice

A crucial feature of these discussions is establishing that no changes will be made in the treatment arrangements by child, parents, or therapist without thirty days' notice. All child analysts have experienced painful summary withdrawals or premature terminations, unilateral announcements of reductions in frequency of sessions, and so forth. By setting up a mutually agreed policy to ensure thirty days to work together before any change, we have found that many treatments can be saved. This is particularly important in work with adolescents, who often use attendance as an expression of conflict. With time to work on the issues, as well as the incentive that the sessions will have to be paid for anyway, most parents engage in the work of examining the problem. The idea of thirty days' notice concretizes the seriousness of the mutual commitment that parents and analyst are making.

Regular Meeting Times

In line with the treatment goal of development along the line of parenthood and consolidation in the phase of psychological parenthood is the provision of separate, regular meeting times for the analyst with the parents. Just as the child's times have to be respected in order to underline the separateness of the child—that is, the parents cannot dispose of them or use them interchangeably—so the parents' times are important parts of the schedule.

Different Modes of Communication with Parents

Regular meetings are not the only methods of ongoing communication and work with parents. Many ingenious arrangements are possible to maintain a collaborative working relationship. As with anything else, however, these alternative modalities may be misused and should be assessed with that possibility in mind.

Telephone Calls

Each therapist feels differently about phone calls from patients outside working hours. Most child or adolescent therapists, however, accept the necessity of being available for urgent contact and the reality that parents may need to call between sessions. We initially encourage parents to contact us whenever they feel the need, as we know that support for parents at the right moment may help prevent domestic strife that can render parents very guilty and ashamed. As treatment progresses, news of a very significant family event or of dramatic happenings that day at the child's school can help a therapist listen differently to material in the child's session, allowing in turn for new avenues of work on the child's communication or lack thereof.

If a parent calls very frequently or demands long, intense conversations, that is a useful signal for the analyst to take up in a parent meeting the level of upset as possibly indicative of a need for the parent's own treatment in addition to the parent work. Similarly, it can open up a family communication problem that needs to be addressed in relation to the overall goal of improving parent-child relationships and interactions between parents.

When the patient, usually an older adolescent, has parents living far away, the telephone is often a help in reassuring the parents about their child's beginning treatment with someone the parents have never met. Under those circumstances, we obtain the adolescent's permission to talk with their parents on the phone and plan the agenda for the conversation with the patient.

Uses and Abuses of E-Mail

One technique now available with the spread of electronic communication is e-mail contact between analyst and parents. This is not a substitute for meeting regularly, but it can serve several important purposes. Offering parents the opportunity to keep the therapist informed of what is happening frees time in meetings from catching up on news, a problem that is familiar from once-weekly therapy. Thus the traditional information-gathering function of contact with parents can often be better served between parent sessions. From the therapist's viewpoint, e-mail is more efficient than phone calls, demanding less time and accessible at the therapist's convenience.

Perhaps even more important is the feeling of access and participation that e-mail contact gives parents. It addresses worries about exclusion and seems to relieve anxiety. Often parents can refrain from angry interactions with children because they know they can write the therapist about the situation. On the other hand, if parents fall into using e-mails to the analyst as "tattling" on the child or as an effort to justify their own reactions, we then take up in the regular meeting their externalization of authority and their nagging or complaining relationship to the child. E-mails often reveal patterns that emerge more slowly in discussion.

Different therapists vary in their degree of responsiveness to e-mails from parents. It is important to remember that any explicit response that addresses the content conveyed by parents lacks the nuance and emotional resonance of face-to-face discussion or even a phone call. Therefore we are conservative about addressing the issues raised by parents through e-mail. It can be very helpful to anxious parents, however, to have their observations validated by the analyst's confirming similar perceptions.

> Six-year-old Frances struggled to maintain distinctions between real and pretend in her play and her understanding of the world at home, in

school, and in her analysis. Her father e-mailed the analyst that he noticed Frances acting anxious and distracted, unable to finish sentences or listen well, and described her having a nightmare about a cartoon character the night before. He was worried, since she had been making good progress. The analyst responded that day by first acknowledging father's increased sensitivity to Frances and then reminded him that this kind of regression had happened once before when Frances had seen a scary movie. The father e-mailed back that he didn't know of her seeing anything recently.

The following day in a parent session, however, the parents reported that they had checked with Frances' grandmother. In fact she had shown an inappropriate video to Frances while babysitting. They told the analyst that the speed of the e-mail communication had helped them address the problem quickly and had spared both Frances and them unnecessary confusion and distress. The parents had been able to talk to Frances about the scary story, and her flare-up of symptoms abated immediately.

With divorced parents who are not seen together, parent sessions may be set up at lesser frequency than ideal. In those situations, the therapist can be kept up to date and each parent can maintain a connection to the treatment through e-mail.

Questions about what information to share arise repeatedly for children, parents, and therapists as treatment progresses. Many different patterns are devised, and often the guidelines change over time within one case. Talking with parents at the beginning about the goal of better communication with their child allows this to be a legitimate topic throughout. In this way, therapists are more easily able to take up family secrets, conflicts over what is appropriate and relevant to share with children, and children's resistances to taking responsibility for discussing their own actions and perceptions.

Analysts' Problems at Recommendation

Making a recommendation for intensive treatment is not easy for analysts. When we do this, we are making an enormous demand on a family and committing ourselves to a long and complex relationship of uncertain outcome. We all struggle with estimating the degree of a child's need and capacity for treatment and his parents' potential for engagement and change. The multiplicity of variables and unknowns can be daunting and includes internal resistances and reluctances in the analyst (Ehrlich, in press). This can be especially difficult for those in training, who have not yet had much experience of the benefits of analysis. How can we develop conviction that analysis is the treatment of choice and that it offers genuine hope? An extended evaluation functions to provide some information about these questions. It also forges a working relationship with parents, which will be crucial to the success of the treatment. Knowing we can work together, sharing some successful interventions, pinpointing where further work is needed, and enjoying the prospect of better understanding the child, the analyst can build on this experience to carry him through the ups and downs of the treatment.

The specifics we have mentioned are all based on the establishment of a beginning alliance between parents and therapist, a relationship of trust and cooperation. Without this foundation, any working arrangements or lack thereof will be quickly used as a resistance and may threaten the treatment.

THE BEGINNING PHASE OF TREATMENT

Being With and Physical Separation

The therapeutic alliance task of parents in the beginning phase of the child's treatment is to allow the child to be with another person. This new person is a relative stranger, in the parents' eyes a powerful stranger who has skills to turn the child against the parents. Thus parents' conscious or unconscious anxiety is no less than the loss of their child or the loss of the child's love. The reactive defense or resistance evoked by such deep fears often takes the form of externalization, usually onto the child. In this chapter we will describe interventions designed to help parents regain their primary parental love so that they can set aside their own pathological use of the child for defensive purposes.

Many different conflicts emerge in the context of the first sessions. The therapist's task in relation to the child is to feel with the child, to discern the conditions under which the child can allow himself to be with this new person. But the therapist's task is also to achieve empathy with the parents in their struggles to achieve their phase-appropriate levels of functioning.

Including Parental Competence and Love

To the extent that the parents' immediate fears and wishes around losing the child express longer-term problems in their own personalities, so will these conflicts be part of the ongoing work throughout the treatment.

Often these fears relate to difficulties in loving between parent and child. Caught in the controlling interactions and rage of a closed-system, sado-masochistic relationship, parents may obscure or even lose their primary parental love. We assume that primary parental love is there in all parents, if only as a potential. Most parents seeking help are already indicating that growth-enhancing, open-system love is more than just a potential. It is the therapist's task to help parents find and maintain their love. Equally, parents often feel unloved by their child and fear that the child will love the analyst better. These parents feel like failures, incompetent and unlovable.

Technically, we address these issues indirectly by working in the parent sessions on all their areas of competence with their children, as well as directly by exploring their own histories as they relate to feelings about the child, including transferences to the child that might interfere with loving. The importance of including all aspects of the parent-child relationship was illustrated in the early weeks of work with five-year-old Henry.

> Henry had greeted the evaluation process and the eventual beginning of his treatment with enthusiastic relief. He was pathetically eager to solve his problems, both to alleviate his own distress and to allay his mother's irritation with him, and charmingly delighted at the idea that he and the analyst would have to work as a team to sort things out. The first few weeks of his treatment saw an elaboration of his preoccupation with fantasies of violent dismemberment and death and a corresponding diminution in his daily life of both symptoms and anxiety—everyone was very pleased. But the parents were prone to attribute Henry's swift improvement, out of relief, to unrealistically exaggerated talents of the therapist.
>
> This idealization of the analyst by the parents was a clue to their ongoing defenses against feelings of unworthiness and hostility toward the therapist.
>
> On the days that Henry imagined the goriest stories, he frequently had to visit the waiting room to check with his mother. By putting together his behavior and the parents' attitude, the therapist concluded that the parents' guilt and feelings of failure were still likely to interfere with Henry's motivation and their allowing him to be with the therapist and enter into the therapeutic work.
>
> In parent sessions, more details of the parents' feelings of similarity to Henry were explored, and the therapist shared with them some general

indications of Henry's accounts of their skills. Henry's talk was peppered with references to his dad's prowess in many fields. His father, however, plagued with lifelong self-doubt and frequently criticized by his wife, had no sense that Henry admired and wanted to emulate him, that he wanted to learn to wrestle and be a champion as his father had been in college. The therapist's account of Henry's adulation was greeted at first with disbelief, which gradually changed to tears and touching astonishment and joy. The father became increasingly interested in spending time doing things with Henry, which was a gain in itself. But it also had direct repercussions on the therapeutic alliance with the parents, in that the father's regaining of his loving tie to his son helped reassure both parents about their primary importance. As they felt more secure in the primary loving relationship with their child, they felt less threatened by the therapist and by Henry's growing attachment to his treatment. They could consider that they also had beneficent effect, not only guilty responsibility for his pathology. As this was worked on, Henry's ability to stay in his sessions and tolerate his own anxiety with the therapist increased visibly.

Issues of separation and loss of love between parent and child, even though addressed during the evaluation, continue throughout therapy. Henry's parents were able to allow him to start treatment, but their conflicts over separation and control were easily triggered. By attempting to control his analysis, they tried to maintain their illusion that there was no separation between them and their child.

Several weeks into Henry's treatment, he contracted a minor febrile illness and suffered extreme night terrors for three nights in a row. His parents were horrified by the gory content of his fevered talk during these episodes and by his lack of memory of them in the morning. Their anxiety infected Henry: the mother was afraid that this proved he was psychotic, his father worried that treatment had stimulated increased anxiety, and Henry decided that working in his treatment was not so much fun after all. The situation called for delicate negotiation: on the one hand, the parents needed reassurance and support, but on the other they needed to be reminded that their son's disturbance would not yield easily and quickly. In their identification with the boy, they had always rushed to shield him from the slightest distress, with resulting increase in his fear of his own feelings. Thus it was difficult for them to face that

Henry would inevitably suffer in the course of his treatment. When they began to understand this, they had to be restrained from urging, even trying to force, Henry to bring problematic issues into his treatment—it was hard for them to let him work at his own pace. The analyst had to address their need to control linked with their anxiety over separation and fear of loss of love.

In parent sessions the analyst said that they seemed to be working awfully hard and worrying a lot about loving and being loved by their son. If they gave themselves credit for their devotion in working to help Henry, they might be able to take their love for granted. Then they would be less anxious and less likely to do things that would interfere with the revitalization of their love for each other.

In the sessions with Henry, the therapist conveyed to him that his defenses would be respected, but would also be addressed—not rushing him with prematurely deep interpretations, but reenlisting him in the task of examining why it was so hard to talk about anything painful or humiliating.

Separation Problems

Young children's separation problems may represent an already longstanding accommodation with their parents. Separation anxiety can usually be traced to a feeling that one is unloving and unlovable. It can indicate to the therapist the presence of an externalizing relationship between parent and child, one in which the child is carrying an aspect of the parent's personality and control is the substitute for love. Externalization is the opposite of loving attunement and is a central mechanism in sadomasochistic omnipotent functioning. Externalization is abusive in itself and can allow for physical and sexual abuse (J. Novick and K. K. Novick 1994). These issues are crucial in confronting pathology in parent-child relationships. In 1970, we described the powerful pathogenic effect of parental externalizations (J. Novick and Kelly 1970). Recent infant mental-health work and therapy derived from attachment research use somewhat different vocabulary but confirm these findings (Warshaw 2000).

Addressing in the parent work the child's difficulties in being with the therapist contributes to the long task of reassignment of aspects of the personality and differentiation between parent and child. In such a situation, we explore the problem with the child and help parents to understand the child's experience. This gradual sorting out eventually allows the parent to face his or her own contribution to the problem; at that point, the young child can usually manage in the treatment room without a parent.

> Marietta, at six, could bear to stay with the therapist only if the door was kept open. This was identified first as her condition for being with, then named as problematic, in that it was accompanied by worries. As child and therapist explored the issue gradually, over months the door was progressively pushed closer and closer to being shut. At the penultimate stage, it was open by the width of a pencil. Regular parent work throughout this period led to resolution of mother's fears of Marietta being sexually abused that stemmed from her own childhood experience, and only then could Marietta shut the door completely.

The separation problem may have expressed this mother's need to use Marietta for her own psychological purposes, but parents who bring a child to treatment have also a powerful wish to free the child for forward development and may welcome progressive moves with joy and relief.

Externalization of Aspects of the Self

A different problem arises when parents and child are locked into a relationship based on the parent's externalization of important aspects of the self onto the child. The term *externalization* comprises a variety of mechanisms in which a person attributes a part or parts of the self to another. All clinicians are aware of the many manifestations of these mechanisms, whether they understand them theoretically as derived from the earliest psychoanalytic explorations or have learned about them from modern attachment theory, attribution theory (Shaver 1985), or the various object-relations theories. Our earlier work in this area (J. Novick and Kelly 1970) explored four of the varieties of externalization that may be used defensively: generalization, attribution of cause or blame, externalization of denigrated or hated aspects of the self, and externalization of the drive or projection proper. We described in detail the distinction between the latter two in the context of family dynamics and consequent variations in technique. In later work (J. Novick and K. K. Novick 1994, 1996a, 1996b, 2000, 2001; K. K. Novick and J. Novick 1998), we noted the use of externalization at the beginning phase of treatment as a way of "being with," added the idea of externalization of *idealized* aspects of the self to defensive externalization, and discussed the distinction between an "externalizing transference" and a "differentiated transference." We see externalization as a central mechanism in the formation of sadomasochistic relationships with their core omnipotent beliefs (J. Novick and K. K. Novick 1996a, 1996b). Each of these forms of externalization may appear in parents' functioning at the beginning of treatment and needs specific technical intervention in order to allow the child's therapy to progress.

An externalizing parent depends on the continuance of a pattern of externalization for emotional well-being or stability, and the child maintains his role for the sake of keeping the parent's love and closeness, as well as to bolster a defensive omnipotent belief in indispensability to the parent. The danger in this situation is that the child's engagement in a relationship with the therapist may threaten to destabilize the pathological equilibrium of the family. This was the course of events in Tommy's case, as described below. No consistent parent work was being done by the therapist treating Tommy or by the therapist who subsequently worked with his brother George.

> Diagnostic interviews with Tommy's mother during his assessment indicated a woman who could not adaptively cope with her view of herself as damaged, deprived, and castrated. Throughout her life she searched for people upon whom she could externalize these dystonic aspects of herself. All the males in her life, including her husband, were extremely messy and low-functioning individuals. From the moment of Tommy's birth until he came into treatment at eleven, his mother perceived him as only a damaged, stupid child.
>
> At the time of referral, Tommy was a prime illustration of what has been called a "self-fulfilling prophecy." There was an exact fit with his mother's externalizations. Despite indications of normal intelligence on psychological testing, he was behind in all school subjects. He was a regressed, soiling, snot-eating child with little control over drive expressions. Most striking was his relative lack of overt anxiety, guilt, or shame in relation to his behavior. What emerged from his evaluation was a picture of a severe disturbance with mental pain and conflict rooted in Tommy's acceptance of a devalued self and an inability to integrate any positive aspects with his self-representation.
>
> Outside the immediate family environment, in school and in his sessions, he defended against hurt feelings almost exclusively by external-

izations. Despite Tommy's evident relief when he had called someone else stupid or disgusting, he still could not see himself as clever or competent. A fluctuating and relatively adequate level of functioning could be achieved only by means of conscious imitation, a type of pseudoidentification with peers who showed the positive qualities he could not own for himself. As he later described it, "When I pretended I was John, I was able to score a goal, but when I was myself I fell in the mud."

Within the family, Tommy felt less need to externalize the degraded self, since he maintained connection and importance by playing the role of the devalued, damaged boy. Central needs were met by acceptance of his mother's externalizations, and he realized unconsciously that complying with her need to use him in this way ensured her attachment to him.

The father played an important role in Tommy's pathological development by offering him no alternative solution. He constantly reinforced the effect of the mother's pathology by using the same mechanisms along parallel lines. The father viewed Tommy as stupid, girlish, and damaged and frequently said so to him. Psychiatric interviews with the father revealed the extent to which this view was based on externalizations of hated parts of himself.

As Tommy began to progress, able to get through whole sessions without denigrating either his analyst or himself, it became clear that his family's equilibrium had been largely maintained by his acceptance of the parental externalizations. Slowly Tommy became consciously aware that "they put the bad onto me and then they feel good." As he gradually overcame his primitive fear of abandonment and could begin to integrate positive aspects within his self-representation, his material centered mainly on the sadness of his mother, the chaos in his home, and the madness of family members. He felt intensely guilty for depriving the family of a target for externalizations, something they so obviously needed.

Indeed, as Tommy's positive development became unavoidably apparent, the family was thrown into disequilibrium and chaos. The father took to his bed in a state of panic and confusion. The mother became depressed, disheveled, and disorganized. She consciously described herself as useless and unlovable and made a desperate search for a new person upon whom she could reexternalize.

There was another child in the family, George, three years older than Tommy. Until the time Tommy began making significant progress, George had seemed like a boy with a well-structured ego who functioned efficiently in many areas. In the eyes of the family, including

Tommy, George was a near genius. It was George who was chosen as the mother's new object for externalization of dystonic aspects of her personality. Very soon, the family equilibrium was restored on a reversed basis, with Tommy seen as the near genius and George as the stupid, messy, damaged child. Tommy, no longer fulfilling his mother's most pressing need, then had to cope with the fact that he was an outsider in his own family. As he said, "I feel the odd man out. I feel good, but nobody notices me." (Adapted from J. Novick and K. K. Novick 1996b, 119–22)

Looking back on Tommy's treatment is an opportunity to examine some of the major issues about working with parents of children and adolescents in therapy. Tommy himself benefited enormously from his analysis, but we think that it took longer and the results were less than could have been hoped for because the pathology in the parenting function was not directly addressed. Improvement in the parent-child relationship and the transformation of the quality of that relationship were not set as explicit goals, and there was no structure within which to examine those issues. Each parent's evident individual pathology was addressed sooner or later in their own referrals, but that work only indirectly affected Tommy and certainly was not timely in terms of his developmental needs. George suffered from the shift of the parents' difficulties onto him, entering a long treatment halfway through Tommy's analysis.

Externalizations by Parents and Analyst to Defend against Pain

There are parents who externalize hated aspects of themselves onto their child; there are parents who cannot tolerate separation and "generalize" (J. Novick and Kelly 1970) aspects of themselves onto the child, thereby seeing no differences between themselves and the child; and there are parents who are conscious or nearly conscious of disliking their child or of having little or no conscious emotions about her. All of these presentations involve defenses against deep pain and guilt over not having an *authentic love relationship* with their child. Parents and therapists may both avoid this deep anguish by remaining on the level of blame, recrimination, arguments, idealizations, and so forth.

Mary entered analysis at eighteen following a near-fatal suicide attempt. At the end of the first year of treatment, Mary was still alive, but the analyst's main concern was that she might become psychotic or kill herself. The parents, however, expressed their pleasure at her progress and their feeling that she was back to being a normal girl, and they suggested that she stop treatment. The parental denial of Mary's lifelong distress had been obvious from the beginning of her analysis; more subtle, but increasingly apparent, was their denial of everything individual about her. For instance, she had never had a birthday party of her own, but "conveniently" shared her party with another family member whose birthday was a week later. The gifts she received bore no relation to her tastes or interests. Each year, the approach of her birthday intensified her conflicts; her suicide attempt had been made just after her eighteenth birthday.

Generalization

As a defense, generalization is frequently used to ward off the painful feelings related to separation. Unconsciously, generalization fuses the mental representations of self and other and so undoes in the parent's mind the increasing separateness of the child that comes inevitably with growth. Therapists faced with parental externalizing defenses that are so deeply ingrained and that can be so destructive to the child's development can feel helpless and enraged. In this arena of such emptiness in the parent-child relationship, the concept of an alternative in working toward an open-system relationship of love and respect provides the therapist with a hopeful alternative that is crucial to maintaining the therapist's perspective and capacity for constructive interventions.

Mary's mother always said that she and Mary were just alike. As the scale of her denial of Mary's individuality became apparent, the analyst and Mary began to understand that the mother was attributing to Mary her own actual or wished-for characteristics, irrespective of Mary's personality. As the later work of analysis freed Mary to begin developing along her own lines, it became inescapably clear that she was actually very different from her mother in temperament, cognitive style, energy level, interests, and talents. Each progressive demonstration of Mary's autonomy and independence triggered an irrational response in the mother. With Mary's continued growth, the family's pretense of normality crumbled. Her mother's condition deteriorated, and she became depressed and suicidal, eventually entering treatment.

During the parent work of the early months, the analyst gently addressed the mother's generalization by remarking on Mary's capacities and skills. Mary's excellent academic functioning in a field very different from that of either parent provided opportunities to comment on how specific and particular her talents were. The analyst made sure to relate these remarks to the parents' pride in their daughter, linking Mary's autonomous achievements to the most positive aspect of the parents' love for her and her love for them. (Adapted from J. Novick and K. K. Novick 1996b, 156–57)

Addressing Parental Externalizations

Confronting a parent directly with his externalizations, particularly at an early stage of treatment, may provoke a panicky counterattack, justified especially since the parent is not the designated patient and has not contracted to undergo therapy. Focus on the difficulties of the parental task of allowing the child to be with another adult, coupled with explicit engagement with the parent's constructive wish to be a good and loving parent, provides the initial motivation for working together on whatever interferes with the parent's job of facilitating the child's entry into the treatment relationship. Tommy's parents may not have been capable of responding to regular parent work, but it is possible that addressing his mother's desperation and his father's sense of inadequacy would have helped, as it did in the case of Henry discussed earlier.

Where Is Love?

Henry's parents could be helped to tap into their love for him through the analyst's focusing on pleasurable shared experiences and bringing Henry's love for them to their attention. With some parents, however, primary parental love has been profoundly assailed by the development of pathological sadomasochistic patterns of relating, if indeed it was ever truly available except as a potential.

Kitty's mother had professed deep concern about her sixteen-year-old daughter's future and seemed to feel genuine distress at seeing Kitty as the excluded victim in relationships with boys and other girls. Within a month of the start of treatment, however, the mother called the analyst repeatedly to complain in very harsh terms about Kitty's hysterical outbursts on the phone with her boyfriend. At these times the mother shrieked at Kitty; with the analyst she questioned whether Kitty was getting anything out of her treatment since the girl was still enmeshed in the "inappropriate" boyfriend relationship that the mother was monitoring by talking to other girls at Kitty's school. Since beginning treatment, Kitty seemed to her mother to be even more intractable, and the fights between them were more frequent.

When treatment produces radical disruption of the family equilibrium, it is sometimes possible in hindsight to see that the original referral was a parental response to the child's attempts at progressive development and represented an unconscious plan to externalize parental failure onto the therapist and keep the parent and child close in a continuance of their former relationship. There are several features that can alert us to the potential for such a negative therapeutic motivation. If we deal with them early enough, the precipitate removal of the child from treatment when it has barely begun may be prevented.

We use the regular meetings with parents in whom we begin to discern the operation of a potential negative therapeutic motivation to explore their feelings of sadness, exclusion, and loss over not knowing each detail of the child's experience for the first time. Simultaneously, extra attention must be given to the parents' genuine, specialized, and unique knowledge of the child, and we place ourselves in the position of learning from the parent what he or she has garnered about how the child's mind works, the patterns of his feelings, and the antecedents of his particular style. It is important to be able honestly to point out similarities between parent and child in order to be believed when we must confront the parents with differences they may want to deny. Equally important is the focus on moments of genuine, nonexploitative, open-system love between parent and child. This is a needed contrast to abusive, controlling externalizations that constitute old patterns of connection between parent and child.

With Kitty's parents, the analyst acknowledged how close Kitty and her mother had been throughout the elementary school years and how this had perhaps led to their using very similar ways to deal with feelings—so similar that they may not have realized that they each needed to develop their own "emotional muscles," learning to tolerate and modulate emotions with increased flexibility. Perhaps mother was feeling as smothered by Kitty as the adolescent was expressing how she felt in relation to her mother. The analyst pointed out that her parents' adult capacity to give Kitty space to experience her own feelings and struggle with her own reactions would eventuate in her returning to closeness with her parents from a newfound position of strength—the alternative was the current family misery, with Kitty driven to ever-greater extremes to carve out a sense of autonomy. The analyst also reminded both parents of the fun they had as a family on a recent vacation.

At this beginning stage, where the focus of the work is on the task of allowing the child to be with and love another adult, we may also use the parents' past and current experience of relationships to the child's teachers, other family members, and alternative caretakers to understand together where things went well and where they went awry. Again we see that apparent motivation for having the child in treatment cannot be taken for granted, but must be explored over time, with conscious, explicit effort put into building a therapeutic alliance with parents.

Forewarned Is Forearmed

When a child is having difficulties in being together with the therapist, it is equally difficult for parents, with their many conscious and unconscious motivations, to sustain support for the treatment. We remind parents of our earlier anticipation of potential fluctuations in the child's feelings about treatment. It allows parents to feel part of the process if we can refer to our joint foreknowledge that the child may have long periods of negativity and apparent stasis as part of our work. As we address these fluctuations and work with parents on improving their own being with the child, we find an improvement in the treatment relationship. For parents, the gratification of discovering that change is possible helps to consolidate a commitment to the process that will be needed at later stages.

Parental Reactions to Flight into Health

Many schoolchildren are referred for treatment because of symptoms or behaviors that upset their parents or teachers but cause the youngster no apparent distress. Some, on the other hand, unlike any other group of children until late adolescence, may enter treatment with reports of unhappiness and be apparently eager for help. This motivation usually disappears in the face of the resistances aroused in the treatment situation. Sometimes the child seeks an escape through a flight into health, with a rapid disappearance of both symptoms and suffering and an announcement of cure. Here too the foundations laid during the evaluation phase with parents are crucial to retaining their support for the child's attendance and continued treatment. When the analyst has predicted the child's "resistance cure," the parents can spot it too and stay firm in their position that the child still has work to do in therapy. When parents waver, it is an indication of a need for work on their continuing conflicts over having a child in treatment, which in turn helps to address their problems in parenting.

> Eight-year-old Mandy had begun treatment enthusiastically, but soon began to come in scuffing the walls, leaving the doors open, switching on all the lights, slamming the cupboard doors, and messing things up. She reacted as if she had been physically attacked when the therapist remarked that it looked as if she were very angry. Mandy accused him of lying, of unjustifiably blaming her; she hadn't done anything; it was someone else who had left the door open, scuffed the walls, and so forth. She became enraged and then claimed the therapist had made her angry with his unfair accusations. She said she had not been angry before, but the therapist's saying it had made her angry, and if he would only keep his mouth shut she would never be angry.
>
> Mandy took her rage and blaming home with her, telling her parents how awful and provoking her therapist was. The parents and the therapist could stand firm together because of earlier work they had done in the evaluation on understanding how difficult it was for Mandy to tolerate her own negative feelings. The analyst and the parents had agreed that one of the goals of Mandy's treatment was a greater tolerance for her feelings; everyone knew to expect storms as she approached these problems. With Mandy, the therapist noted how critical she was of anyone being angry. The therapist's curiosity about this attitude soon

intrigued Mandy enough to allow her to begin to explore the nature of the threat posed by anger.

Transferences within the Family

The clinical exploration of intrafamilial transferences, as illustrated for instance in Taylor's treatment described below, is long familiar in both child and adult analysis. Confirmation can also be found in current empirical work that uses the Adult Attachment Interview (George, Kaplan, and Main 1996), which demonstrates the relation between parents' attachment histories and their relationship to their own child.

At some point in the relationship with parents, it is useful to explore their own memories of childhood and gradually consider the ways in which this may color their view of their child. We often start with general, open-ended questions about what it was like when parents were young, with the hope of eliciting memories of constructive, open-system functioning as a potential emotional resource.

But moments of open-system love in the past are not the whole story. Usually it is important for the therapist to engage parents in active exploration of past roots to interferences with primary parental love. The child may represent a sibling, a parent, or themselves. Sometimes this can come up during the evaluation, as we saw with Henry's mother, who worried that Henry would be like her disturbed brother. In other situations, both material in the treatment and family reactions to change in the child bring the current playing out of old relationships into the foreground. Disruptions can be extreme, as we saw with Tommy, where the analyst had no direct access to the parental externalizations. With Taylor, who entered treatment at five, and whose parents were seen regularly by the analyst throughout, the patterns of transferred and externalizing relationships could be discerned and addressed more explicitly.

> Taylor had been brought for treatment at five because of her parents' concern over her apparent fascination and fearful excitement at sexual matters and a lag in reading readiness. Mother and daughter quarreled continually and seemed to be locked in a sadomasochistic interaction. The parents presented a vague possibility that Taylor had been molested by her brother Kenny, who was eleven years older. In fact, her mother

had witnessed many instances in which Kenny grabbed Taylor's buttocks and nipples, licked her genitals, and climbed into her bed at night from infancy on.

After six months of treatment, Taylor started to play out with little dolls Kenny's visits to her bed when she was younger. Eventually she began to talk of his excited behavior, and the analyst could help her clarify the real and imagined effects of Kenny's intrusions and Taylor's attempts to reenact these in her treatment relationship.

Within a year and a half, Taylor made great improvements, particularly in her reality testing and differentiation between self and others. She almost never presented the withdrawn, confused, unintegrated appearance of the early days. Her massive defensive disruption of her synthesizing function and memory had yielded to interpretation and verbalization, and her relationships and cognitive functioning reflected these gains. But, as Taylor progressed, the family showed signs of disruption, with parental discord increasing markedly.

The concrete sexual abuse had taken place in the context of a long and complex family history of dysfunction, in which externalization played a prominent role. Taylor's father had first married a very disturbed woman who abused their children physically and sexually before committing suicide. He then married Taylor's mother, who weighed two hundred pounds at the age of nineteen. She herself had been sexually abused by an uncle in early childhood. Subsequent interviews with Taylor's father substantiated the inference that he related to women as damaged and defective. The line of externalization through generalization came also from the maternal grandmother, who was preoccupied with the idea that she and her daughter should be exactly alike, to the point where she urged her daughter (Taylor's mother) to dye her hair to match her own hair color. By the time Taylor's treatment began, her mother had become slender and had begun to do graduate work, while Taylor was overweight, confused, and sexually abused.

The analyst met with the mother regularly throughout Taylor's analysis, with father joining in when possible and occasionally attending sessions on his own. The historical information about the family, which was very helpful in understanding Taylor, came through this work. In addition, many interventions became possible. During the period of Taylor's working through her feelings about the events with Kenny, her mother was able to understand why it was important to reduce the overstimulation of scary movies; outings that were inappropriately exciting, intrusive, and confusing; lack of privacy in bathrooms and bedrooms; and so forth.

And yet her unconscious participation in exposing her daughter to potential abuse persisted; for example, she bought Taylor a dress that said "Tickle me" all over it. In the interview where this outfit's message was called to her attention, the mother talked extensively about her own mother's pressure on her to be like her. The analyst asked about the maternal grandmother's reaction to mother's childhood sexual abuse. The grandmother had been vague and denied that it really happened. In a similar way, while Taylor's mother was fully aware that Kenny was impulsive and had himself suffered sexual abuse, she had nevertheless denied the clear indications that he was abusing Taylor. At this point the analyst interpreted the mother's need to protect the maternal grandmother from her own rage and reproach as leading her to do to Taylor what maternal grandmother had done to her, that is, externalizing her own helplessness, confusion, and uncontrolled excitement onto the child and identifying with the unprotective grandmother. The interpretation seemed to have a strong impact. Within two weeks, Taylor's mother had resumed her own analysis and seemed genuinely to have changed the tone of her interactions with Taylor. (Adapted from J. Novick and K. K. Novick 1996b, 158–61)

The advantages of regular parent work during the beginning and middle phases of treatment were clear in Taylor's case. The analyst could help her parents recover and maintain their loving, affectionate investment in a child who appeared stupid and dull through the hard early months. The parents helped the analyst make sense of Taylor's sterile and confusing play. As the meaning of Taylor's inhibitions and ego restrictions emerged, there was a danger that Taylor would be retraumatized by ongoing overstimulating experiences. Regular, detailed monitoring with parents of her daily life helped them see the connection between their provision of "fun" and Taylor's feeling of being overwhelmed by impulses. Eventually, on the base of a firm working relationship, the analyst could make an interpretation to Taylor's mother of her continuing unconscious perpetuation of abuse—this freed Taylor's treatment from the drag of her mother's pathology, enhanced differentiation between Taylor and her mother, and allowed the mother to address her own difficulties.

Working with Parents of Young Adolescents

Work with parents is as necessary with patients in early adolescence as it is with younger children, both for current needs and to lay groundwork for a healthy relationship between parents and child in later adolescence. The patient must feel confidence that privacy will be absolutely protected; here the work of the evaluation with patient and parents in setting guidelines for what can and cannot be shared shows its usefulness. At the same time, it is in the nature of phase-specific issues that young adolescents and their parents test the limits of such guidelines, provoke each other into action and reaction, and need consistent help in keeping joint goals in mind. Some families have such difficulty trusting each other initially that they need joint sessions; others find it most helpful for parents to meet regularly with the child's therapist to work on negotiating family decisions, adjusting to the child's new level of functioning, dealing with the adults' reactions to the child's puberty, and riding the fluctuations of the patient's dependency needs. Regular meetings safeguard the therapist's position of neutrality between parents and child and reinforce the continuing importance of the parents in the child's development.

Parental Conflicts

Part of the difficulty for parents of children in this age group comes from the parents' own adolescence. The unavoidable and sensitive issues of a time in life when one's body and personality are changing rapidly, social and interpersonal expectations are in flux, and childhood fantasies must be confronted for integration or rejection were not easy to deal with the first time. For parents of pubertal children, there is the revival of feelings from their own histories, the frustration of watching the child go through them, and the impact of the child's burgeoning sexuality, both directly and comparatively, with attendant implications of parental decline. A first technical approach to these issues in the parent sessions is to ask parents to remember their own teenage years in order to help them differentiate their own experiences from those of their child and to note similarities that may enhance their understanding of the child.

Supporting Parents' Adult Identities

Parents may struggle to remain the idealized successful figures of earlier times to maintain an important source of narcissistic supplies; they may compete with the child, asserting their own sexuality in new flamboyant ways; or they may idealize adolescent functioning and seek to emulate it, just at the time when the child most needs the role models of responsible adult functioning in order to integrate his new growth. Work with the parents therefore seeks to support their functioning in the parental stage of development, which includes their search for sources of self-esteem outside their children's idealizing regard, acceptance of mature sexuality and relationships, and modeling of responsible work and love. We work with them to foster respect for the child's growing individual identity and use the model of our learning from the child in the therapy to help parents regain genuine interest in the child's tastes and activities, rather than curiosity for the purposes of control.

Parents' difficulties in maintaining an adult perspective take many forms. The issue may come to light first through the analyst's reactions to a young adolescent, as with twelve-year-old Nicola.

> Nicola was a depressed middle-school child, daughter of recently divorced parents, who was able to use her unhappiness to punish and control them. The parents alternated between intense feelings of guilt and rage at their daughter for being so pathetic and dumpy. At the beginning of treatment, Nicola presented as a passive, helpless, pubertal girl who often retreated to a state of torpor so powerful and contagious that the therapist found herself uncharacteristically sleepy and distracted.
>
> The therapist focused on Nicola's way of "being with," and they both began to understand that her extreme passivity and helplessness was simultaneously a defense and an attack against her parents, particularly her mother. Parallel with this beginning work in Nicola's analysis, the therapist was exploring with the parents their own experience of being with Nicola. The therapist could respond to their descriptions with genuine empathy for the impact the child's passivity had on others. Without giving a specific account of sessions with Nicola, the therapist talked in general about her experience with patients, young or old, who are passive or helpless. She described how she could find herself feeling helpless too, beginning to doubt her own capacity as a therapist. How much more intense it must be for the parents, when they are also dealing with the aftermath of a divorce and all the attendant feelings of failure, loss, and so forth. Nicola's parents responded by confirming how devastating her depression and passivity were for them, how they felt useless as parents and not much better as people.

The therapist noted that, even under ideal circumstances, the passage of one's child into adolescence brings up feelings about aging and loss and also memories of one's own adolescence. Both parents spoke about their own painful teenage years, and the mother in particular recalled her self-destructiveness and extreme inhibition. Her own parents had divorced at that time, and for the first time she recalled blaming her mother, thinking that when she got married she would never let herself get so fat, ugly, and shrewish. She then wondered if her daughter might be having similar feelings, if her helplessness and disinterest in self-care or socializing were her way of saying that she was no better than her mom. Nicola's mother ended the session saying, "She's entering adolescence and I still have much I can teach her, help her with, support her in. I think we'll start with both of us going to a spa and having a makeover."

Rather than seeing this focus on externals as a defensive retreat from painful feelings, the therapist supported the mother's understanding of the relationship between feelings about the body and the self and her perceptiveness in discerning Nicola's conflicts over competitiveness with her mother.

Working with Parents of Older Adolescents

Parents of late-adolescents are subject to many vulnerabilities. Conflicts from earlier phases in the child's life persist, with the additional elements of the undeniable reality of the child's physical, social, and sexual maturity. Some parents use their child's treatment as the arena to play out these conflicts and pathological solutions to them. Persistent denial of the adolescent's maturity often appears in attempts to control the time aspects of the therapy, with recurrent questioning of the agreed-upon frequency of sessions, duration of treatment, or vacation arrangements. Another arena for the operation of parents' omnipotent defenses is that of money, with forgetting the fee, resistance to payment arrangements that make the late-adolescent patient responsible, pressure to involve the therapist unduly in questions around third-party payments, or even attempts to cut corners or cheat on insurance claims. It is not unusual to have parents of late-adolescents stubbornly insist on handling all practical aspects directly, such as payment, cancellation, frequency of sessions, duration of treatment, and so forth. They can allow their children to have credit cards, go on expensive vacations, make decisions on college courses, for example, but have great difficulty allowing them to be responsible for an analysis.

Manifestations of Closed-System Relationships

Such problems indicate an ongoing relationship between the parents and the late-adolescent where the predominant way of being together has involved control. This mode of relating by the parents is bound to show up in the late-adolescent's entry into treatment, when the elements of the parents' conflicts at each level of development become manifest. Pain and mortification from feelings of failure as a parent, guilt over hostility to the child, wishes for an exclusive relationship, and competitive feelings persist. Late-adolescent development adds a particular challenge to parental denial of mortality: the relative decline in powers and possibilities. Allowing and facilitating their child's entry into treatment is an expression of the progressive, appropriate parental wish to help the young person move forward in life. But these positive, loving impulses need reinforcement so as not to be vitiated by the destructive forces that work to undermine the establishment of a therapeutic alliance between the late-adolescent and his therapist.

Remembering the Special Needs of Late-Adolescents

Neglecting to reinforce positive parental feelings causes many therapeutic failures early in the treatment of young people. One contributor to such a failure is the prevalent pattern of treating late-adolescents as adults, with no explicit provision for the specific needs of parents during this phase of their children's development. If we recall, however, that we have defined the parents' therapeutic alliance task at the beginning of treatment as allowing the child to make a significant relationship with another adult, we can devise techniques that both protect the patient's working toward being with the therapist and address parental anxieties and conflicts over allowing the therapeutic relationship to develop. Part of the discussion of the working arrangements during the evaluation involves planning with the patient for meeting the parents' needs in relation to the treatment. We generally suggest formal sessions with the patient and his parents at regular intervals. Sometimes this is impossible for reasons of geography or circumstances such as hostile divorce. But some provision for ongoing contact is crucial. When there are apparently external reasons for difficulty in building an alliance with parents of late-adolescents, we bring these into the work with the patient, making him responsible for joining in the effort to solve the problem.

The importance of including parents in the ongoing work is exemplified in the contrast between two adolescents, one an eighteen-year-old in treatment with no ancillary parent work, the other a nineteen-year-old with parent work done consistently from the start of treatment at sixteen:

> In the first case, treatment started when the boy was seventeen, because of school failure. His parents were seen only briefly during the evaluation. Jeremy made considerable improvement in the first months of work—he was less depressed, his grades improved, and he was feeling better about himself. He had been smoking marijuana since middle school, and at times he seriously abused the drug, staying stoned for days on end. One day he was caught at school with marijuana in his car, and he was suspended. His father was in a rage. Both parents felt that treatment had been a failure and peremptorily ended his analysis.
>
> Janet also presented with serious school problems, depression, and self-destructive behavior. She too made significant progress, but when she started college she began to abuse alcohol, sometimes becoming "wasted" to the point that she could not remember the events the following day. This issue was being addressed in the treatment when Janet had a serious car accident while driving drunk. Her car was totally wrecked, and she was fortunate that no one was seriously hurt. Her mother was furious and wanted to punish Janet to "teach her responsibility."
>
> The analyst had met regularly with Janet's mother and stepfather during the high school years and maintained contact when Janet started college. The mother called the analyst and expressed her rage and frustration, saying how much she wanted to punish Janet, but said, "I wanted to talk to you first." A series of meetings with Janet and her parents led to working out a reparative program that everyone could feel comfortable with. Most importantly, it maintained the loving, supportive tie between parents and child. Analysis continued, and important inroads were made on Janet's self-destructive rage when she had been left by a boyfriend and on the roots of these reactions in her early abandonment by her father.

The Transformative Aim of Late-Adolescent Treatment

Work with parents during this phase, whether done in regular meetings or through the adolescent, can focus on the task begun during the evaluation phase of transforming the relationship between parents and adolescent from one of defensive control and antagonism to one of mature cooperation, pleasurable mutuality, and objective love. We remind the parents and the adolescent that one goal of treatment is to allow them to develop a loving, mutually enhancing, evolving relationship that reflects and respects the changing needs of all participants. Since parents are sure to have difficulties with their task of allowing the adolescent to be with the therapist, they may need repeated reassurance that the therapist is neither a parental replacement nor a competitor. The treatment relationship is unique; its aim is therapeutic, and the ultimate goal is restoration to the path of progressive development, which includes a satisfactory relationship with one's parents. In the safety of a clearly defined, distinct therapeutic relationship, the analyst may observe the dynamic patterns among family members and make explicit the obstacles to progress in development.

> Ben was a nineteen-year-old sophomore in the musical theater department of a local college. He was the youngest of three sons, ten years younger than the next oldest. There was clearly an underlying story about his conception since he had no idea why there was such an age gap between him and his brothers. From early childhood he had shown marked talent in singing and dancing; in third grade he set his sights on a Broadway career. He was the lead in all his school productions; won places each summer at highly competitive performing arts programs; and had already, despite his youth, played the lead in the department's annual major production.
>
> This department was very good, but not the best to which he had been accepted. His parents had insisted that he was too young to live farther away and that he had separation problems, and they implied that they could not afford the tuition at a better school. However, the two older brothers had been fully supported in their college studies at prestigious East Coast universities. This pattern was established early on; for many years resources were poured into supporting the two older boys, but the youngest had them grudgingly doled out. This had been

an issue during the evaluation, when Ben's parents had balked at paying for intensive treatment. Despite their awareness of his serious depression and the availability of an unusually generous insurance program, they haggled over the fee and the frequency of sessions. They agreed to have Ben start treatment out of concern at the suicidal potential as his depression deepened and because the analyst suggested that the entire situation could be reevaluated at the end of the school year, seven months on.

Ben responded quickly. His depression lifted, and the story emerged of his being controlled, teased, and depreciated by his adored older brothers who were clearly envious of his talents. The parents seemed to have done nothing to protect him, but went out of their way to minimize his achievements and compensate the brothers for his success. Ben was convinced that any success would evoke envious attack from his brothers and lack of protection or collusion from his parents. He began to articulate his feeling that he was an unwanted stepchild, who could remain part of the family only by blunting his talents and curbing his desires.

At this point the therapist suggested a meeting with the parents and told Ben that he wanted to explore this pervasive dynamic and find out the reason for the age gap between Ben and his siblings. Ben was invited to attend, but he declined, as he worried that his parents would feel inhibited by his presence. At the meeting the parents expressed their relief at Ben's recovery and wondered if treatment could end in a few months. The therapist acknowledged their relief, but said that he was concerned by an emerging picture of Ben's stopping himself from fully succeeding. The analyst talked about the impact of the brothers, their envy and hostility toward Ben's success, Ben's love for them and fear of hurting them, and Ben's love for his parents. He added that their support of his treatment and their evident relief at his recovering better spirits testified to their love for Ben. The parents seemed very moved by this comment, as if no one had ever articulated love between Ben and his parents.

The analyst then asked about the age gap—was there a story behind the ten years' difference? Both parents blushed, stalled, and said that there was still pain and confusion around that issue and they would rather not discuss it. They said that they had talked about this in their own therapy, so it was dealt with. The analyst said, "I understand your reluctance to talk about something painful, but this is something that may help Ben—it is the brave and responsible thing to do. Sharing it with me so that I can better understand Ben is important, and it will probably eventually enhance your relationship with him." The mother said, "He's right. It's like a boulder in the road; we need help to move it." She told of a time when the marriage was in a crisis; the father was having an affair, and they were heading for divorce. She had thought that a baby might bring them back together, so she had tricked her husband into having unprotected intercourse and she conceived. She said, "I think that Ben always reminds me of that terrible time and of my deception." The father at first denied ever thinking of it, but then remarked thoughtfully, "I think I always resented Ben, as if he had stopped me from staying young forever."

Ben's mother laughed and said, "Is that why you had the affair?" The father answered, "Didn't you know? You think that young airhead could hold a candle to you?" They laughed, she cried, and they left holding hands after promising to talk to Ben about those troubled times.

His parents had seldom attended Ben's performances, even though they did not live very far away, which hurt and confused him. Work in his treatment addressed his responsibility to interest them in his current life and achievements and his conflicts over including them and telling them how important they were to him.

A few years later the therapist received a note from Ben. It contained a newspaper clipping praising his performance in an off-Broadway musical. At the bottom, Ben wrote, "My parents were at the opening. For this and other things, many thanks."

Structuring Joint Sessions with Parents of Adolescents

Various techniques can be used, but we have often found it helpful to restrict the content of joint meetings with parents and adolescents to discussion of current issues—for instance, use of the car, course selection, financial support, vacations, and so on—so that any irrational patterns of interaction will emerge. The therapist describes the patterns, which gives parents the possibility of changing and provides material for further work in the adolescent's treatment on transforming the relationship to parents. The resistances that arise in relation to this effort to establish the therapeutic alliances among all parties in the beginning of the treatment once again help us to understand the terms of the patient's conflicts.

Internalizing the Relationship with Parents—Becoming a Parent to Oneself

A crucial developmental task of late adolescence is the internalization of the positive relationship to parents so that the young adult begins to parent himself well and eventually becomes capable of parenting others. As we examine the obstacles to the patient's being with the therapist, including those that come from the parents' conflicts over allowing the therapeutic relationship to develop, we illuminate the patient's difficulties in establishing benign, constructive internal parenting functions. In working together on establishing the therapeutic alliance with parents, the patient and the analyst come to examine how he has internalized pathological aspects of parenting. We begin also to be able to see how the patient colludes with maintaining the status quo of a controlled and controlling relationship with his parents, both the real ones of the present and the internal representations from the past. Two styles of dealing with control conflicts can emerge, as they did in the contrasting situations of Courtney and Lara.

Courtney's wealthy family provided expensive holidays and gifts for everyone in the family, but the first response to any request of Courtney's, whether reasonable or not, was always a refusal on financial grounds. Money was the ultimate leverage in her family, and payment for her treatment was no exception. Courtney was expected to beg for support for treatment, college, and more frivolous activities and feel grateful and guilty when her pleas were granted. She made elaborate plans about timing and wording for approaching her parents without ever questioning the basic premise of her total childish dependency on her parents' permission for each small purchase.

Making the initial arrangements for her treatment had involved numerous long-distance phone calls with her parents, each of whom wanted to make a different deal with the analyst, and neither of whom wanted to have Courtney take any part in the discussions. The analyst made a firm statement about the interference Courtney's difficulties posed to her completing college and appealed to the parents' wish to have an accomplished, capable daughter. With repeated assurance that they had produced a child who could indeed manage with the help of treatment, the analyst secured their grudging agreement both to analysis and to Courtney's handling billing and payments.

Lara presented herself in each session in a guarded, constricted way. Her way of talking about daily events seemed drained of feeling, as if she were dutifully informing the therapist, but experienced no pleasure or relief in sharing her life. Lara's parents had put a very large sum of money in the bank in the autumn of Lara's first year of college and told her she was henceforth responsible for all her expenses, including treatment. Lara was suddenly cut loose without ever having been taught even to balance her checkbook and with no practice or advice on budgeting or making financial choices. Lara's constriction and inhibition of being with her therapist were understood as a defensive response to her fear of feeling overwhelmed by helplessness. She felt unsupported internally, as she had not yet taken ownership of parental functions.

Since Lara's parents had made it very clear that they no longer wanted to be involved in her daily life, it was not possible to work on these issues directly with her parents. The work took place in Lara's treatment, where she and the analyst could work together to analyze Lara's conflicts over acquiring life skills.

It is often around these issues of parenting oneself that the late-adolescent first becomes aware of how few life skills have been imparted or how comparatively independent his peers really are. Work with parents in such situations can focus on the enjoyment they will find in sharing their knowledge with their child, developing a close relationship on a new level. Support and reinforcement of their pride in the adolescent's ability to handle paying the rent, sticking to a clothes budget, and so forth is crucial to their continuing growth as parents of a young adult.

Differently Structured Families

The task for parents at the beginning of treatment is to allow their child to be with a stranger. In this chapter we have described some of the anxieties and defenses inevitably evoked in parents under these new, stressful circumstances. The situation can be even more intense when there are additional factors for the family and therapist to encompass. Although each situation is unique, we know that every circumstance has an impact that has to be taken into account. Thus it is important to know the family history and the circumstances of the child's beginnings so that every relevant influence on parents' and children's functioning can be included. It matters to children, albeit differently in each case, whether they have two mommies or two daddies, or only one parent or grandparents bringing them up; whether the family is blended by divorce and remarriage or by combining biological children with adopted; whether one parent is disabled or chronically ill; and so forth. When the child is adopted, there is a wide range of practices, such as open or closed adoption; foreign or domestic adoption; interracial, biracial, or cross-racial adoptions; and early or late placement, each with its own psychological ramifications. Children are sometimes conceived with the aid of newer technologies, such as in vitro fertilization or the use of fertility drugs, which may now include an agreement to "cull" fertilized ova. With these techniques, there is a variety of permutations in becoming a parent, such as single parents with unknown donor, single parents with assistance from family donation, lesbian parents with one undergoing artificial insemination or IVF, male partners with one donating sperm, and so on. Each of these situations carries important meanings for the parents involved.

Parent work with differently structured families warrants fuller attention in its own right, but here we can indicate how our model applies. The assumptions we discussed in chapter 2 hold regardless of how people become parents. The main point is that parents are crucial to children's development and crucial to successful passage through each of the phases of treatment. All parents have hopes, concerns, anxieties, and sensitivities that must be understood and worked with. These inevitably evoke myriad counterreactions in therapists. In our supervisions and consultations, as well as in our own work, we have found that diverse family backgrounds also elicit further specific conscious and unconscious feelings and beliefs, which can affect the therapeutic work. This could be seen in work with an adopted five-year-old girl treated by a younger colleague.

Nadia started analysis at five with a lifelong history of angry protest and temper tantrums. She had been adopted at birth, and her parents found her charming but exhausting. The mother was at the end of her capacity to tolerate Nadia's furious outbursts; she felt guilty but powerless over her wish to withdraw from Nadia. Nadia began her treatment by telling her analyst that she was hungry. The analyst responded by giving her sweet snacks, which became a daily feature of the sessions. Treatment proceeded with important insights that helped Nadia gain greater emotional stability and control as she explored her fantasies and fears around her birth mother, and Nadia attended enthusiastically.

One day, however, the analyst disappointed Nadia by not having purchased a particular toy she wanted, and Nadia erupted in rage, saying she was a bad doctor who didn't understand what was important to little girls. Nadia's mother heard the yelling from the waiting room and at the end of the session remarked to the analyst with some evident satisfaction, "Now you finally know what it's like!"

Following consultation with one of us, the analyst realized that everyone—mother, child, and analyst—had been playing out a fantasy scenario related to Nadia's adoption. The mother had never truly engaged with Nadia's sadness and anger, as she did not feel entirely legitimate as the parent; she was not helped by parent work to feel secure in her parental position, so ordinary competitiveness with the analyst had not been addressed, but instead had been exacerbated. The analyst had responded to Nadia's "hunger" as a "better mother," with the usual rescue fantasy increased by an unconscious sense that, for an adopted child, anyone can indeed be the mother. This dynamic had blocked her usual skill in picking up negative feelings in the therapeutic relationship. Nadia had used the availability of the analyst defensively to split her ambivalence to her mother and ward off dealing with the mental situation of having two mothers represented internally, which is a predicament all adopted children have to come to terms with. With the realization that issues around the adoption had been playing a powerful, but inadequately addressed, role all along, the analyst could reengage more directly and fruitfully with Nadia and her parents in the reality of their current family structure.

One of the most difficult aspects of working with families that have what may be considered potential extra loadings in their histories is assessing the significance of these factors. Just as parents struggle to gauge the impact of their particular circumstances on their parenting and their children, so do therapists struggle with the pull to explain too much on the basis of specifics of the background or to collude with parental wishes to deny consequences.

The mother of two little girls, very close in age, consulted an analyst when the children were four and five years old. Both were conceived by artificial insemination from the husband's sperm, as he was confined to a wheelchair because of injuries suffered in a catastrophic accident before his marriage. The father had made extraordinary and successful efforts to maintain mobility and independence, which were profoundly important to him and much admired by his wife. Both children had a variety of symptoms, including fears for their parents' safety, leading to intense separation anxiety, and eating and bowel issues. To the analyst, all of these seemed likely to involve the children's reactions to their father's disability, but the family had been steadfast in a shared determination not to let any of his limitations affect their functioning as a family. A long period of parent work with mother and father, seen separately and together, was needed to come to a shared realization that it was important for the girls' development that their parents help them integrate the realities, both positive and negative, of their father's situation. Father accepted a referral for individual therapy, and both girls eventually entered treatment during the school years for their internal conflicts over their own capacities and achievements.

In some ways it is easier for a child to grapple with visible disability in a parent. Chronic illness may have as profound an effect on the parent-child relationship, but the manifestations may be more disguised, as we saw, for instance, with eight-year-old Karen, referred for incipient school phobia.

Karen's mother suffered from severe lupus, with pain and debility that could keep her bedridden for days at a time. In short periods of remission, she was relatively pain free, but struggled with anxiety over the uncertainty of recurrence. Karen was a serious, competent child, good at her schoolwork, capable in self-care and physically healthy, as well as kind and caretaking of others. She was puzzled by her worries about going to school, as she liked school, but felt that she really needed to be home with her mother. Work with Karen focused on her anxieties and her wish for omnipotent control in circumstances where something no one could control so governed her family life.

Parent work with Karen's mother, with father's occasional attendance, consisted largely of discussion of what and how much to explain to Karen. The mother worked through her own guilt and sadness at the impact of her illness on her daughter. Then she felt much freer to be matter-of-fact when she needed Karen's help, as well as to intervene directly when she thought that Karen was reversing roles and taking too much care of her. These parents were helped in a relatively short treatment to find a comfortable baseline for understanding that mother's illness meant many different things to Karen and that both parents could help her by delineating explicitly what the illness was and wasn't and what differences it could and couldn't make to Karen.

In addition to different family structures and circumstances that have special impact on children, all therapists deal with cultural differences among families and between any one therapist and families, which are more or less distinct. We have many such experiences in our practices and teaching, as well as in the diverse range of families, drawn from a multiracial, multiethnic community, that attends our local psychoanalytic preschool.[1] The assumptions underlying our model of parent work in the clinical situation apply to considering sensitive differences in many settings.

There Are No Easy Answers

The brief vignettes and technical suggestions above may not adequately convey either the detailed difficulty of parent work or the extent of some parental pathology. It is hard even for therapists to accept the darker dimensions of parental feelings and stay mindful of parental hate and destructiveness to children, even while seeking to enlist the healthiest parts of parents' personalities in the therapeutic alliance. Deep-seated parental pathology, expressed in the use of a child for psychic survival, can emerge at any point in the treatment and may or may not be successfully dealt with by the analyst. The techniques that issue from our model of working with parents, rooted as they are in the tasks of the therapeutic alliance and theory of the two systems of self-regulation, are not a guarantee against failure but an aid in this truly most difficult part of child and adolescent work.

The theory of two systems of self-regulation gives us the idea of alternatives to closed-system, sadomasochistic beliefs, defenses, relationships, and actions. This supports the therapist in having confidence that parents can find solutions different from omnipotent guilt, externalizing defenses, rage, and wishes for revenge—defenses against deadness and trauma.

Indications of the Beginning of the Middle Phase

There are numerous markers of the shift from the beginning phase of treatment to the middle. These involve qualitative changes in the tone of the work with the child or adolescent patient, with an increase in comfort between patient and analyst and shared interest and focus on workings of the patient's mind and feelings. The alliance task of the middle phase involves working together and demands maximal use of ego functions by both parties to accomplish the work. For parents, to the beginning-phase demand of tolerating *physical* separation from the child, there is now added the task of supporting and enjoying the child's growing *psychological* separateness, the individuation and autonomy of the child's first steps toward changing her personality.

This is a moment of potential pride and shared joy, but it is equally a time of danger of premature, unilateral termination of a child's treatment by the parents. They may experience their child's growing psychological independence as a physical or psychological loss. Parents may use the child's symptomatic improvement as the reason for stopping, and so avoid making the transition to supporting autonomy.

The Need for Empathy with Parents' Sadness

Child analysts, who tend to identify with the child, may get very angry with parents at such a point, feeling that the parents are sabotaging the child's efforts to use the treatment to grow up. It is crucial for the analyst to be able to empathize with parents' fear and sadness in their belief that any separation, physical or psychological, means losing their child or his love. Here the prior work during the evaluation and recommendation bears fruit in our being able to remind parents that our goal is not only to restore the child to the path of progressive development, but also to transform the child's relationship with parents to one of closeness on a new level. The following vignette illustrates how a child's increasing autonomy can revive parents' earlier anxieties about actually losing him.

> Damian, ten, was so sad and constricted at the beginning of treatment that he told the analyst he thought his family would be better off without him. He was an only child, much loved by his high-achieving parents, whose

standards were impossibly exalted for both themselves and Damian. Prior work with the parents helped them to set more realistic goals and enjoy Damian's increasing relaxation. But, as he began tentatively to pursue his own intellectual interests instead of their ambitions, they started complaining about the burden of treatment. Now that Damian was not overtly miserable, they wanted to stop. The analyst agreed that Damian was indeed looking happier on the outside and reminded the parents of their earlier shared treatment goal of fostering increasing freedom of Damian's thinking and creativity, as well as a flourishing relationship with his parents. The analyst wondered about the parents' plan to have Damian cut short his pursuit of his own creative interests.

The transformations that had been worked on during the evaluation and beginning phases included Damian's parents realizing that many of their feelings had an impact on him. The mother spontaneously wondered what it might be in her that was creating such pressure to bring the treatment to a premature close. The therapist asked if she were again afraid she was going to lose a child. This intervention was based on the therapist's association to material in the developmental history about the mother's miscarriage before Damian's birth. Her response, however, was a surprise. She cried and said, "Like I lost the other two." She then explained that she had an abortion when Damian was under a year old because she thought and had been told that it would be too difficult to manage two infants. "It was the worst mistake of my life." In subsequent work, it became clear that Damian stood as a double replacement child for her. The parent work became emotionally intense over the next few months as they used the sessions to talk about and mourn the losses, but there was no longer any mention of ending Damian's treatment prematurely.

Treatment Threatens Externalizations

Parental externalizations can interfere both at the beginning and in the move to the middle phase, as parents depend on the physical or psychological proximity of the child to maintain their own defensive equilibrium. The work of the middle phase challenges the mutual accommodations made by parents and child on the basis of externalization and internalization. Work with Helen illustrates how past experiences around a child's increasing autonomy and psychological separateness led both parent and child to expect and fear criticism and loss of love.

Helen was eleven years old when she started analysis because of her extreme and unremitting upset at her parents' separation and imminent divorce. The mother was in therapy and was eager to start treatment for her child as soon as possible. It took considerable work to help her see that a precipitant of the referral had been her own feeling of helplessness in relation to her husband, her sense that she was incapable of protecting herself and her daughter from his emotional abuse. A further reason for the mother's urgency that did not emerge until much later was that Helen was a tall, physically precocious girl who had been visibly pubertal for at least two years and had just started her periods.

The analyst did not begin Helen's treatment until the mother could understand that the analyst would not function as a bodyguard, but would help her use her own capacities to be the kind of parent she would like to be. During the beginning phase she could, with support, help Helen to be with the analyst in the face of father's open opposition to the treatment. At first the sessions with Helen contained constant threats; withholding, stubborn resistance; and angry words. Gradually there was a shift to quiet games of cards in which both Helen and the therapist could share and look together at her difficulties, such as her appearing and acting stupid when she was really very smart, an overwhelming need to win even if it meant cheating and lying, and in general finding very little pleasure in the way her mind worked.

The first sign of Helen's transition to the middle phase effort of working together with the therapist came via her mother's subtle acting out of resistances: she brought Helen slightly late or paid late. These reactions were signals for the therapist, but were too subtle for the mother to accept as having any meaning. Soon, however, Helen began to use her mind actively in the sessions and began talking about events at home. She had initially acted like a "ditzy valley girl" to fit in with pathological externalizations of both parents, but as she began to differentiate herself from their expectations she used her keen perceptions to criticize her parents, especially her mother. She told her mother things the analyst had said in such a way that the mother felt attacked. Helen distorted and misused the therapeutic work to make her mother feel denigrated by the therapist. The mother became very upset, went to her own therapist to complain and blame herself, but said nothing to the child's analyst.

In a parent session at that time, the analyst commented to mother that, although Helen was beginning to use her mind more consistently, she seemed unsure if it were safe to do so and seemed to be showing this by being somewhat provocative and hostile, which the analyst could understand might be hard for the mother to tolerate. Mother then reported the accusations that Helen had attributed to the analyst. This allowed for the emergence of her feeling that the analyst was unfair. When the analyst commented that mother might well be feeling angry, helpless, and abused, she began to cry. For the first time, she recounted her own experiences of continuous and severe emotional abuse as a child, when she had been treated as a "dumb blonde," never respected for her own opinions. She was helped to see that Helen was struggling to use her own perceptions and use her own mind, rather than accede to the image of the dumb blonde or become the abusing male bully her father was. The mother's task, in parallel to Helen's, was to use her indignant feelings as a signal to mobilize her intelligence for understanding what was going on in Helen, rather than as a panic button to shut down her thinking and endure in confusion.

This accomplishment in the therapeutic alliance with the mother was reflected in a shift in Helen. In the sessions, work moved away from her complaints about mother and other outside factors to her own sadomasochistic fantasies, confusions, and anxieties, especially around boys, pregnancy, and childbirth. During this time, the analyst commented on her growing curiosity and wish to learn and know, in contrast to her need to pretend she knew nothing. "I don't do that anymore," Helen said. In the same session she talked for the first time about her admiration and envy of her mother's achievements. In the next parent session, work continued on mother's pleasure and pain in seeing Helen growing into a different kind of person from mother. The analyst could then share with her Helen's growing appreciation of her mother as a separate person and point out that this was a basis for a new kind of relationship between them.

The analyst could also point out to Helen's mother that being different did not lead to being criticized and unloved. Then an interpretation could be made that perhaps both mother and child carried the belief that love could be maintained only by being the same and never leaving each other.

Divorced Parents

Helen's parents' divorce was a major factor in her troubles. Children of divorce are disproportionately represented in clinical populations. In those families headed by a recently divorced single mother, there is a high risk of early interruption or unilateral termination of the child's treatment (Rembar, Novick, and Kalter 1982). Many factors contribute, but it is clear that particular care is needed in techniques of working with parents under stressful circumstances where treatment and the therapist may be used as transference or displacement objects or to meet genuine current needs.

Functioning as a Parental Conscience

We think that it is best for the child to feel that both parents are involved in her treatment and support it, but this is not always possible. Adversarial parents can sorely try the neutrality and equidistant stance of the analyst. It is often necessary to see parents separately or to accept that one parent will not participate in the treatment. We explain to parents that their child needs someone who is actively not taking sides in order to feel safe enough to bring all her different feelings about each parent into therapy. This stance allows us to speak up firmly when we feel that parental fighting is frightening or confusing a child—we have temporarily established ourselves as a parental conscience at a time when parents may be preoccupied with their own hurts and battles.

Helping Divorced Parents Work Together

In work with divorced parents, we do not try to get them to agree in general or to reconcile them; nor do we do couples therapy. We acknowledge that there were indeed many reasons that they divorced, but stress the importance for their child that they work together as parents. We emphasize their continuing responsibility for parenting and suggest that our goal together can be to make them the most effective parents they can be, despite divorce and its attendant complications.

Nine-year-old Larry was the third of three children in a divorced family. The parents had recently finalized a very disputatious divorce and settlement and could barely tolerate being in the same room together. They came for help because Larry had no friends, was doing poorly at school despite high IQ test scores, and was generally miserable. At the first meeting, they soon lost their focus on Larry and began blaming each other for their pain and troubles. Each was in an individual analysis but seemed to be using that work to confirm the view that the other was at fault for everything that had happened.

After ten minutes of a rising crescendo of mutual accusations, the analyst stopped them and said that the divorce was over and need not be replayed. As much as they might hate each other and not want to interact in any way, they remained Larry's parents, and their presence demonstrated their deeper valuing of that important role. She noted that in a divorce the child loses the security of the parental couple, a sense of two people working together to care for him, love him, and meet his legitimate needs. The therapist said that in order for Larry to feel loved it was essential that he feel that his parents still worked together to do what was best for him. She suggested they first find areas of parental agreement between them. For example, it seemed clear that they would both like him to do well at school, have friends, and feel better about himself. They should focus on these areas of convergence, make them explicit to Larry, and if possible enlarge the domain of positive co-parenting.

The parents were taken with this approach, but then quickly fell back into blaming and accusing each other. This time the analyst intervened quickly and said she could feel their hurt, anger, and disappointment. But they had their own analyses to deal with their issues. With this intervention the focus could remain on Larry and his need for positive parenting. On this basis the evaluation could proceed, and treatment soon started. Larry's parents were seen separately on alternate weeks and together once a month.

Larry responded well to his analysis; his initial symptoms abated, and by age eleven, at the start of middle school, he had become a competent, successful, and psychologically separate boy. His self-esteem was still precarious, and he struggled with acknowledging and channeling his lifelong rage at both parents for not being available to meet his needs as he was growing up.

His parents were pleased with his progress. Larry's mother thought he was ready to finish; his father was uncertain. The fact that they disagreed was used as a spur to explore what might be going on with Larry. In her own parent session, the mother and the analyst talked about her fear that Larry's increasingly critical stance with her meant that he would want to leave her and go to his father. The father admitted that he still felt angry with his ex-wife and might be using his son to get back at her. Mother realized that Larry's being angry and critical did not mean that he would stop loving or needing her.

Work with both parents elucidated the confusion they shared that being a separate person meant denigrating and leaving one's parents as they had each done in adolescence. With this uncovering work accomplished, the parents could again work together to support and validate Larry's forays into separateness. Larry could more freely move ahead into the middle phase of his treatment to explore the unique workings of his mind and body.

Single Parents

These techniques also help us avoid the pull to make parent work with a single parent into a general psychotherapy. We keep in mind the therapeutic alliance tasks with parents of a child in treatment, as well as the treatment goals that relate to transformation of parental functioning and the parent-child relationship. Then the work with a mother or father can focus on parenting issues, and a simultaneous referral for their own help can be made.

The Impact on Treatment of Marital Dysfunction in Parents

Parents do not have to be actually divorced for their marital dysfunction to have a long-term pathogenic impact. As treatment of a child proceeds, the role the child has been cast in as preserver of a dysfunctional marital relationship may become clearer. Progress in the child's treatment may upset a long-standing, delicate equilibrium in this realm, just as we saw in terms of shifts in parental externalizations. The child's part in maintaining the status quo may become dramatically visible, as it did in the case of Luke.

Luke, who nearly died following a suicide attempt at sixteen, had been in treatment for a year when he and the therapist remarked together on the improvement they noted in their joint capacity to track Luke's fluctuating states of being with or distancing himself from the therapist and the therapy. The focus of the work was shifting to the ego functions interfered with by his "zoning out" and the consequent additional conflicts and bad feelings. Zoning out, with or without the aid of drugs, was increasingly linked in sessions to specific content and feelings, particularly anger. One effect of this work was a significant change in Luke's feelings about himself. He said that, for the first time since he could remember, he did not feel depressed. He had plans, hopes, and could at times even feel proud of himself.

In the regular meetings with Luke and his parents, the insight had been achieved that good feelings in Luke were often followed by some family member precipitating a crisis or battle. After Luke and the therapist had shared Luke's newfound level of satisfaction, they both thought it was important to have a meeting with the parents as soon as possible. During the telephone call to arrange a time, Luke's father remarked that he had noticed that his son seemed to be happy for the first time ever. Two weeks later, halfway through the time scheduled for the family meeting, the mother called the therapist to say that at that very moment Luke was on a plane to a "therapeutic boarding school." The parents had arranged that as Luke walked out of the house to come to the meeting with his therapist two men had seized him, had taken him to a waiting taxi, and had put him on a plane to a destination the mother had been instructed not to reveal, particularly not to Luke's therapist.

This devastating event was a dramatic demonstration of a breakdown in the therapeutic alliance with the parents of a late-adolescent. Despite the work already accomplished, the crucial transformation of the problems, from interpersonal interactions among family members to Luke's own internal conflicts, had proceeded more rapidly with Luke than with his parents, and they were unable to tolerate the anxieties evoked in them by his progressive moves.

Impact of Physical and Psychological Separateness on Parents

The timing of this disruption, at the transition from the beginning to the middle phase of Luke's treatment, can elucidate typical features of both phases. As Luke became more comfortable and less conflicted about being with someone other than his parents, they reacted with a violent retrieval of complete physical control. Thus we may see that issues of loss and physical separateness, of individuation and autonomy, are salient to the therapeutic alliance tasks of the beginning and middle phases of treatment with both patients and their parents. We may expect that conflicts will emerge as changes take place in the patient on these dimensions. As Luke began to use his ego capacities more consistently, entering into the middle phase of treatment with its emphasis on the task of working together, he was relinquishing long-standing identifications with parental externalizations of helplessness, misery, and failure. The depth of the parental need for maintenance of externalizations onto the child becomes apparent in the impact of the patient's increasing involvement in working together.

A year later, when Luke returned from the boarding school, he insisted to his family that he resume treatment. Clear agreements were made among all parties that the treatment would not be summarily interrupted. Luke made steady improvements in all areas of his functioning. When Luke first started treatment, his mother had expressed her terror at his unbridled rage. Indeed, Luke had caused physical damage to their house and furnishings during his outbursts. As analysis resumed, his mother expressed continuing fear of him, although Luke had actually gained considerable mastery over his impulses. The first focus in the resumed parent work was on Luke's improvement, with ongoing work in his analysis on his need to sabotage his gains. The analyst noted in parent sessions that Luke seemed to be figuring as a different person in his mother's life story, being an actor in someone else's play when he behaved impulsively or lost control. Over the next few months, Luke's father noticed that his wife began to pick on him whenever she felt positive about Luke. Father was dismayed by this realization, as it made him aware of how little he had protected his son from the mother's anger, perhaps out of self-defense. Throughout the remainder of the treatment, Luke's father was a consistent ally in support of Luke's progressive development.

The analyst could then begin to note explicitly in the parent sessions that they kept describing Luke as a threatening male, even though he no longer behaved in this way. After initial defensiveness, Luke's mother revealed for the first time that both her father and her brother had been physically abusive. The analyst used this material to underscore and promote differentiation of Luke from past figures in the parents' lives. Luke and his parents built upon this to establish better boundaries between them.

A further effect of this work, however, was to highlight the dysfunction in the marital relationship and each parent's pathology. The healthier Luke became, the more his family fell apart. His mother broke down, his father had affairs, and his younger brother became addicted to drugs, thus confirming the earlier insight that Luke played a central role in the family's dynamics as an object of externalization for all members. Even during the family crises consequent on the breakdowns in other members, however, the work done around Luke's differentiation held. Each parent sought individual treatment at this time, and each also noted that their growing positive recognition and pride in Luke was crucial to their capacity to stay together as a family. This work made space for Luke's analysis to explore his own self-destructive conflicts. Parent work during the rest of the treatment often included Luke and consisted of meetings designed around specific issues, with the analyst working to ensure the safety of Luke's growing autonomy and the consolidation of positive communication and respect in the family.

Notes

1. Allen Creek Preschool is an award-winning nonprofit psychoanalytic preschool in Ann Arbor, Michigan, a founder member of the Alliance of Psychoanalytic Schools.

CHAPTER SIX

THE MIDDLE PHASE OF TREATMENT

In the last chapter, we noted that the transition from the beginning to middle phases can be a peak of resistance, with the danger that parents will unilaterally end the treatment. However, once parents' deep fears of loss of their child and of his love can be addressed, children and adolescents usually settle into the long middle phase of work exploring the intrapsychic world. In many therapies this has been the time when parent work, if done at all, is set aside or diminishes to meetings a few times in the year for informational catching up. Therapists may prefer to turn their attention to the unfolding of the child's inner life and can experience parents as irrelevant or a hindrance.

The Importance of Middle Phase Alliance Tasks to Treatment Outcome

Our view is otherwise. We suggest that the middle phase brings with it a series of important tasks in the alliance with parents that, if engaged with, can consolidate the adult in the phase of parenthood, can allow for dealing with subtle parental resistances that can stalemate the child's treatment, and can help ensure that the therapy will proceed to a useful termination with continued positive growth beyond the end of treatment.

The alliance task for parents in the middle phase of treatment is to allow increasing psychological separateness, individuation, and autonomy. These, however, threaten parents with feelings of abandonment, loneliness, and loss of love and can represent an assault on basic aspects of the parents' personalities. To deal with these anxieties, parents may withdraw from their child, work to protect their own character defenses and superego structure from any impact of the changes in the child, and resist revival or revision of past experiences.

By the middle of a treatment, parents who have worked consistently with the child's or adolescent's therapist through the earlier phases have addressed their extreme feelings of failure and transformed their guilt into usable concern. They have begun to regain a sense of competence as parents and can begin to see their children as separate from themselves, which allows for starting to master the tasks of psychological separation from the child and permitting the patient to be with another adult and to begin to form a significant relationship.

Middle Phase Alliance Tasks

As noted above, allowing for psychological separateness, individuation, and autonomy is the primary task for parents during the middle phase, accomplished by working collaboratively with the therapist. We look for parents' increasing ability to facilitate and enjoy the child's or adolescent's separateness by supporting the child's new ways of being and new adaptations, including more adaptive ways of coping with internal and external stresses. Parents are learning to balance the sadness of their feelings of loss with respect, love, and pleasure in the child's growth. They become open to pleasant surprise at the child's new interests and blossoming talents, joining the child in new modes of relating.

Parental Anxieties in the Middle Phase

The middle phase of any treatment brings with it a deepening of material and increased complexity of dynamics. This is certainly true in child and adolescent therapies; the addition of parental conflicts and resistances, and their interaction with the child in treatment, makes the therapist's work ever more challenging. The therapeutic alliance tasks during the middle phase bring specific anxieties, conflicts, and defenses in the parents, which can give rise to resistances, stalemates, and premature termination. We can characterize three problematic parental dynamics that will probably have to be addressed in the middle phase. One is parental decathexis or disinvestment of the child, followed by withdrawal or displacement. The second is parents' protection of their own personality structures, particularly characteristic defenses and superego configurations. Children are often drawn into or collude with this defensive protection. Third is parental resistance to the revival and potential revision of issues from their own histories.

Reactive Parental Withdrawal from the Child

The child's or adolescent's increasing psychological separateness confronts parents with their own personality limitations, often reviving painful issues from their own pasts. The child's growth can represent a massive assault on the adult's characteristic defenses, superego configurations, and modes of dealing with painful or traumatic experiences. When the therapist engages the parents during this phase of the child's therapy, there is a risk of a major counterattack. Conscious or unconscious worry about this may contribute to a therapist's avoidance of continuing parent work. Parental self-protection may not necessarily take a blatant behavioral form, however, but may appear as a withdrawal of investment in the child.

> Eight-year-old John, the child of divorced parents, was sometimes brought to his sessions by his father. There was a lot of giggling, wrestling, and physical contact whenever they were together in the waiting room. During the first year of treatment, the therapist had worked with John around new ways of making friends and doing better at school. The therapist noticed that every time father brought John he entered the session regressed, provocative, and unable to work. When his mother brought him, he functioned at his most advanced level. In John's session, the therapist remarked on this contrast and wondered aloud if all the physical activity with his dad was upsetting to John. John denied this in the session, but asked his father to stop wrestling. In the next regular parent session, John's father told the therapist that he thought his son didn't love him anymore, but that he didn't mind so much since he had his younger son and could now love him.
>
> In this situation the therapist could clearly track the sequence of the oversexualized, pathological mode of relating: John's effort to separate

himself from his father's use of him, the withdrawal of investment in John by the father, and the subsequent reexternalization of excitement onto his next child. First the analyst questioned the father's assertion that John did not love him. Father's belief that love is equivalent to sado-masochistic enmeshment (closed-system love) could be made explicit. Father then volunteered the memory that this was the way he related with his own father and older brothers.

The father and the therapist then began to explore other ways of loving more in tune with John's own interests. For instance, he took John to a car dealer with him when he was shopping for a new car, and they shared their likes and dislikes. The relationship began to change to a warmer, more age-appropriate interaction. Soon after this, the father asked for a referral to begin his own therapy while continuing in parent work.

Sometimes, however, parental withdrawal is more subtle. The parents do not oppose the treatment and seem cooperative. The initial worries of the beginning phase seem over, the child is improving, and the analyst may feel that there seems to be little need to meet with parents. We have come to think that this feeling may indicate a danger point. In the middle phase, we are dealing with issues of psychological separateness, a major source of conflict, anxiety, and defense for everyone. If parents or analyst feel there is nothing more to talk about, this should be as much a signal of difficulty as more extreme reactions to progress. Cases such as that of Luke, the adolescent described in the last chapter, whose parents kidnapped him when he began to change, have alerted us to pay particular attention to parental reactions to the child's or adolescent's initial moves toward autonomy and to note whether they are absent, subtle, or more extreme. We try to address them quickly.

In a meeting a week after the analyst had described to her parents how eight-year-old Amy was beginning to work things out on her own in treatment, the mother looked depressed. The analyst noted this mood and invited her to talk about it. At first, Amy's mother denied feeling "down." Then she said she had been "feeling a little logey" and wondered if she might be getting the flu. When the therapist then said that actually she sounded sad, the mother's eyes began to tear. "You're right," she said, "I hadn't noticed it, but I do feel sad, and I don't know why." After they explored together some other possible sources, the analyst remarked

THE MIDDLE PHASE OF TREATMENT

that they had talked the previous week about an important growing-up step taken by their daughter; the analyst noted that it is quite usual for parents to react to their child's forward moves with pride and pleasure, but also with sadness.

The parent session ended with mother feeling much lighter, but the next week she said that she was continuing to struggle with periods of sadness. "I feel as if I've lost something; I don't know what." The analyst suggested that they think together about autonomy and what it meant to the parents. Amy's mother and father talked about their own experiences in adolescence when their parents had reacted with rejection and hostility to their growing independence, treating them as if they were abandoning the family. As they described the guilt and anger connected with these issues, the analyst helped them realize that they had internalized their parents' reactions and were repeating their own attachment histories with Amy.

This difficult and powerful therapeutic work began to address an intense conflict for both of Amy's parents. On the one hand they felt the need to maintain a sense of connection with their own parents, bolstered by externalizations, and to defend against guilt at potentially surpassing their parents, avoided by pathological generalizations. On the other hand, they deeply wanted to create a space for their little girl to blossom and to feel good as parents. Without direct work on these issues, parents desperately protecting their own characteristic defenses might have prematurely terminated Amy's treatment.

Avoidance of Parental Conflicts Produces Stalemate

Even when a treatment continues, there is a serious danger of stalemate in the child's therapy if the therapist avoids addressing central parental conflicts. Amy's parents, in their fear and anger that her independent growth constituted a hostile rejection of them, consciously or unconsciously created Amy's (and every child's) worst nightmare—that they would emotionally withdraw from her and abandon her. Children who pick up this danger usually react with their own version of withdrawal, retreating from the therapist and the therapy, since both represent autonomous progressive development. This can take the form of apparent compliance, as we saw in the case of Damian, the very sad ten-year-old.

113

We noted earlier the intensification of the parent work when Damian's mother revealed her secret history of double loss. Equally significant was the corresponding shift within Damian's therapy. Despite his increasing comfort and security in the sessions, there had still been a quality of rapid compliance with the parents that made it hard to discern the distinction between his psychic space and theirs. It was only after they could begin to see that they had externalized aspects of their own history that Damian began to talk in his own sessions of ways in which he differed from his parents and how angry he felt when they assumed that they knew his wishes.

Protection of Parental Defenses

We have earlier described interactions between Henry's difficulties and his parents' problems involving both externalizations and pathological identifications. Another issue arose in the middle phase.

Henry's own therapy was proceeding, with work focused on his anxiety about bodily integrity, when his father complained bitterly in a parent session about Henry's "lying." Father felt that Henry, by then nearly seven years old, constantly evaded the truth to avoid responsibility for his chores and homework, that Henry blamed others when he lost his backpack or jacket, and that Henry kept "fudging" the difference between real and pretend. The analyst agreed that these were serious issues and talked to the parents about how boys at this stage struggle over a developing conscience and how thinking and perception are sometimes drawn into intense conflicts. In this context the analyst noted in a general way how important it was that his parents be clear and consistent about rules and realities.

Henry's mother said she had been trying but felt unsupported by her husband on this dimension. He indignantly protested when she detailed his flouting of rules and laws in front of the children, deciding arbitrarily when they should wear their seat belts, riding his bike without a helmet, changing Henry's bedtime unexpectedly, and so forth. The analyst reminded father of how closely Henry and he were identified with each other and suggested that perhaps they also shared a problem about their consciences. Henry's father became quite angry and stopped coming to parent sessions for two months.

At the next meeting, the analyst apologized to Henry's mother for apparently touching a nerve with her husband. The mother did not want to talk at any length about it, although she seemed embarrassed by his absence and made an excuse for him. Rather, she was preoccupied with a surge in Henry's anxiety level and his reluctance to go to school. The analyst took her lead and focused for the next several sessions on understanding together how Henry's deep worries interfered with his capacity to use his ego to differentiate real and fantasied dangers. Then they moved to considering how mother could help Henry enjoy the security of a predictable routine and expectations. As Henry relaxed within the safety of a more consistent daily experience and both his mother and his father could see the difference, Henry's mother felt stronger in being able to advocate with her husband for an effort to set a better example. Henry's father returned to parent sessions and rejoined the work directly, more able to think at least about his son's developing superego.

Working in Displacement

This experience in the work with Henry and his parents shows how easily a challenge to a parent's superego configuration can potentially derail a treatment. In retrospect, it seems that the analyst moved too quickly into drawing the parallels between Henry's and his father's conflicts. The father reacted with angry defensive withdrawal, and Henry's anxiety surged; without the mother's deep and somewhat desperate commitment, they might have stopped treatment at that point. The analyst then worked with Henry's mother explicitly to develop alternative solutions to Henry's troubles with his conscience. They looked together at the cost to Henry of anxious, hostile, and self-punitive functioning and the visible gains of freer experimentation within a framework of safety. It was very important that the analyst help the mother to see the parents' central importance as models and containers for Henry for her to have her positive role validated. It would have been better if this could have been done with both parents directly, rather than initially through the mother, with the added demand on her that she convey these ideas to Henry's father. Focusing the parent work on children in general, with the understanding that one is also working in displacement on the parents' difficulties, calls for the same kind of patience, restraint, and timing that we use in individual work.

Working with and through Only One Parent

Sometimes, however, the pathology or character issues of one parent may be such that it is impossible to work directly at all with both parents together. Rather than a temporary hiatus, as with Henry's parents, the analyst may have to work with and through only one parent for the whole time of treatment, as was the case with four-year-old Davey.

> Davey's idealized father had left the family when Davey was two. Despite the severity of Davey's aggressive and anxious symptoms, his father was vehemently opposed to treatment from the start. He refused to participate in any parent sessions, with or without his ex-wife. Davey's mother persisted, however, and made the decision to proceed with treatment. In the middle phase, it was apparent that Davey greatly enjoyed his treatment and was changing visibly, including developing a clearer sense of himself. That in turn meant he saw his parents more realistically and had better inner controls. His father demanded that the analysis should stop right away. The father also began to criticize the analyst to the child and tell Davey that he shouldn't go there any more. The analyst's efforts to have father come in to discuss the issues were fruitless.
>
> From what the analyst could discern, the interaction between Davey's parents was similar to the sadomasochistic battles Davey engaged in with his mother, in which she played the passive, helpless victim while covertly enraging Davey further. Mother constantly badgered her ex-husband to pay for Davey's treatment, although he had always refused and didn't actually have the resources. Rather than be rendered helpless and furious in this situation, the analyst suggested to the mother that she explain to Davey's father that the treatment would end much sooner if he supported it emotionally. She would not ask for financial support if he offered positive validation for Davey's own experience, but she would legally petition him for back child support and his financial responsibility for his child's treatment if he prolonged the treatment unnecessarily by putting the child in such an impossible loyalty conflict. Davey's father backed down and began to remark appropriately to Davey when he noticed him controlling his anger and excitement, attributing the changes to the hard work Davey was doing with his analyst.

This was a situation in which the sadomasochistic character pathology of both parents was so severe that it had to be addressed by confrontation. They had played interchangeable roles of bully and victim during their marriage, and these persisted in their parenting afterward. The work with Davey's mother throughout the treatment had, however, expanded her repertoire of realistic responses and healthy investment in her child. This allowed the analyst to work with her to support her addressing her ex-husband's destructiveness directly.

Sacrifice of the Child and His Treatment to Parental Needs

The outcome is not always so positive when middle phase work threatens long-standing role relationships in a marriage or family. A family secret that can no longer be denied, or abuse in the past or present, can become the focus of intense parental efforts to maintain the status quo and resist the impact for change that comes from a child's treatment. We have written about the negative therapeutic motivation (J. Novick and K. K. Novick 1996b) with which a parent brings a child to treatment in order to make the analyst fail and to preserve a pathological, usually externalizing, relationship. We can now extend this idea to include the parents' effort to use the child in a new way to protect a pathological family structure. In open-system development, parents and children change with each other as each develops into new phases. When a family has found a pathological equilibrium, it can be disrupted by developmental changes or external imperatives, like school entrance. A perversion of the developmental process occurs with a reconstitution around new sadomasochistic patterns, as we saw in the case of Kenny.

Six-year-old Kenny had suffered from his mother's screaming rages and his father's wildly sadistic teasing and overwhelming through most of his life. When he entered treatment he was unable to stay alone in a room, toilet himself, go to school, or sleep in his own bed. He also could not be left alone with his little brother without attacking him mercilessly. After a year of analysis with weekly parent sessions, Kenny had greatly improved—he was attending school, had mastered toileting, could play at another child's house, and woke only a few times in the night. This excellent progress had been achieved through analysis of his murderous terror and its underlying omnipotent belief in the power of his aggression, and through painstaking parent guidance around basic issues of routine and respectful interchange.

What had not changed much was Kenny's mistreatment of his brother and his parents' embarrassment in front of their friends and family at Kenny's relatively high anxiety level about anything and everything. The parents' emphasis on how humiliated and ashamed they felt elicited the analyst's empathy, as well as a sense that such intense embarrassment intimated the fear of having something exposed. In exploring this, both mother's and father's rage at Kenny for making them "look so bad" emerged with renewed force. It was as if the ordinary guilt they had felt, that had been worked with throughout, was just the top layer. Underneath was a certainty that they really were going to be shown to be terrible parents, that this devastating possibility might really be true. This fear masked an omnipotent conviction and wish that they had a right to use Kenny as they wanted. They had spoken of many incidents of humiliating Kenny with teasing—father always shook his head ruefully, telling the analyst he knew he would get in trouble in the session for these things. Mother had cried over her knowledge that screaming at him only made Kenny more scared.

The analyst had worked with the parents around their household organization in which mother felt unsupported because she carried full domestic responsibility while father worked very long hours and pursued a time-consuming hobby outside the home. Matters came to a head when father went on one of his frequent business trips, leaving mother alone with two difficult small children and no household help, although the family could well afford it. Kenny's anxiety peaked whenever his father was not there to protect him in the night. Kenny acted out in school, and the teacher called mother in at the end of the day in front of other parents. She was humiliated and enraged, feeling that she and her child were singled out and, at the same time, that Kenny deserved severe punishment rather than the understanding she felt was counseled by the analyst. When father returned, he confined Kenny to his room, which produced angry, hysterical panic and tantrums. The exhausted child finally went to sleep, but father woke him for school by pouring cold water over him in bed, which produced another panicky outburst.

Despite feeling very angry, indignant, and worried about Kenny, the analyst was able to see that mother felt helplessly overwhelmed and that father was in the grip of a compulsion he could not control. The analyst tried to elucidate for them the impact of their handling on Kenny and what was understood from his sessions, but parents were adamant in their stance that Kenny was the villain of the piece. Another tack taken in the parent work was to support mother in her articulation of her practical and emotional needs, in parallel with Kenny's work on saying in words what he felt and wanted.

At this juncture Kenny's analysis had proceeded to the point where old structures within him were shifting, but this meant he was rejecting blanket externalizations from each parent, was protesting when his autonomy was attacked, and was seeking alternative sources of gratification outside the sadomasochistic interaction within the family. His parents could not tolerate the changes this demanded from them. Kenny was too important as a repository for externalizations to their individual personality structures and to the secret abusive power gratifications within their marriage. Rather than risk exposure and the attendant demand to change, they sacrificed Kenny and the treatment, removing him summarily.

Resistance to Revival

As treatment progresses and parent work produces greater insight into the history and causes of the current troubles, many parents suffer deeply over their faults of the past. A major issue in parent work during the middle phase touches on the distinctions between shame and guilt and between remorse and regret. When a person functions predominantly in the reality-based open system, doing something wrong triggers shame, then remorse. Remorse is a feeling that accompanies open-system functioning, in that it recognizes the reality of our helplessness to undo the past.

In contrast, for someone who omnipotently and unrealistically feels responsible for things beyond his capacities, wrongdoing produces guilt, often followed by externalization of blame or fantasies of revenge to get the unbearable feeling outside the self. Regret arises later in this sequence, with its implication of the omnipotent capacity to deny the reality of time and go back to undo the original fault. When it becomes possible to set aside the omnipotent quality of the feeling of guilt, a person is left with remorse. With remorse, reparation becomes possible. In a family context of real sins of omission or commission in the past, reparation can be considered in terms of what can actually be done currently (J. Novick and K. K. Novick 2004).

Reparation

Despite the limitations of reality, parents can be helped to take a series of reparative steps.

CHAPTER SIX

Acknowledgment

First there has to be an acknowledgment to the child of past wrong-doing. For instance, we can help a parent to recognize that even being a passive bystander while someone else was abusive allowed the abuse to occur. As we saw in the partially failed case of Kenny, this is often done to protect oneself or the marriage. This emerged clearly also in work with the adolescent Luke.

It was an important and dramatic period in the parent work when Luke's father faced that he had stood passively by. He had sacrificed his son for his own safety and self-defense. His wife accused Luke and treated him like a monster in the service of her rage against men. After a period of work on her relationship with her son, Luke's mother turned her rage onto the father, threatened divorce, insisted that they sleep in separate bedrooms, and stopped coming to parent sessions.

Soon after this, the father called Luke's analyst in some distress. He said that he could not sleep for thinking about what he had allowed his wife to do to Luke. What could he do? At this point, Luke's analysis had slowed down, with Luke missing sessions or zoning out during them, especially at moments of work on his anger with his parents. Luke only occasionally had access to his rage at his father—he said his father was still being passive. Father and son were uncomfortable talking with each other, usually provoking disputes. Each would leave conversations feeling angry and disappointed.

The analyst responded to the father's plea by suggesting a joint session with father, Luke, and therapist. The meeting started with Luke looking sullen and father unable to meet his eye. Father then began to talk about his realization that he had not only left Luke unprotected, but had done it for selfish reasons, because he was afraid of mother's rage. Luke seemed startled at first, but then retreated behind a wall of words, complaining that it was "too little, too late." Father mumbled "I know," and slumped further down in his chair.

The therapist noted that father's acknowledgment had taken some courage and was important as a first step. Father straightened up and began to talk. He noted his inability to undo the past and apologized with deep sorrow and regret for what his son had endured because of him. He looked at Luke and said, "I have always loved you, but I think my actions, or rather inactions, made a huge wall between us. Can we try to become friends now?"

Luke sat silently for a while, then said, "I think I have always hoped you would say this, but more, I also hoped you would rescue me, go back and make it never have happened. I guess I have to give up that magic wish." Tears came to both their eyes as Luke said, "This is good." Both men were "tough guys" who had always blanked out rather than show any feelings. To the surprise of all three in the room, they reached out for a handshake, then rose to hug each other, and both cried for the rest of the session. Luke and his father no longer needed the therapist's active presence in joint sessions to continue to work on developing their relationship.

Addressing Current Effects

A further reparative step that the analyst can encourage is parental awareness of the continuing impact in the present of past events and sensitivity to related current difficulties. Then parents can do something ameliorative in the present. After the work described above, Luke and his father could react together to current conflicts and Luke's self-destructive behavior in a different way.

> Another effect of this parent work was to break the deadlock in Luke's own treatment. He began to reflect on his continuing need to see himself as the victim of an abusive mother. Luke wondered if this kept alive his magical thoughts about being rescued. He said, "I could probably keep this up forever, but what's it getting me? It's an endless cycle of suffering, getting overwhelmed with rage, zoning out, and then having to work so hard to come alive again. It's a waste; I have too much I love to do."

In these illustrations we can see some of the complexity and challenge of parent work during the middle phase and how it requires of the analyst all the skills and techniques acquired in work with both children and adults.

Parent Work and Confidentiality in the Treatment of Adolescents

In earlier chapters we described a hierarchy of clinical values, with safety and the best interests of the child paramount. Confidentiality comes afterward, although it is an important component of creating security in the therapeutic relationship with children of any age. Here these considerations are joined by issues specific to the treatment of adolescents. The most powerful argument made against concurrent work with the parents of adolescent patients grows from the version of psychoanalytic developmental theory that defines the development (and treatment) goal for adolescents as separation from parents. It follows from this point of view that any overlap, cross-fertilization, or integration of individual with parent work could breach the increasing distance being established between the young person and his parents. One analyst of adolescents remarked in discussion that recommending parent work with adolescents was like advocating a diet of hamburgers and french fries to a heart patient—one cancels out the other.

In our view, the goal of adolescent development and hence of treatment is not separation, but transformation of the parent-child relationship and integration of the new self-representation. In relation to parents, the goal is to transform the relationship into one that can incorporate the realities of biological and psychological change in adolescence and middle age. Physical separation, as when older adolescents go to college, is not necessarily the best or only method for accomplishing these goals; indeed, physical separation may work to solidify pathological, closed-system methods of self-regulation or delay open-system transformative growth. Unfortunately it is the external physical separation of college entrance that has taken on the cultural status of the rite of passage into adulthood (DeVito, Novick, and Novick 1994). This traditional Anglo-American reliance on physical separation to accomplish psychological tasks has been incorporated into psychoanalytic theory and then reexported into mainstream culture so that parents and adolescents alike expect young people to want to leave, be completely separate, and have secret lives that their parents do not know about or even feel they have any right to share.

Working as we do in a town with several large colleges, we have been faced with this attitude that has profound impact on the issue of parent work when adolescents are in treatment. How do we negotiate this territory when so many parents have explicitly defined college as a time for their children to "sow their wild oats" and "have the best years of their lives," and when they have said they "don't want to know" what is going on? Our understanding is that such socially validated secrecy actually retards development as it allows young people to rebel without directly confronting parents and to simultaneously avoid taking responsibility for their own actions. This culturally determined notion that adolescence should be a time of secret rebellion often takes the form of getting drunk to the point of indulging in indiscriminate sexual activity and then being unable to remember one's actions. In this context, both parents and adolescents worry that the wall of confidentiality as secrecy will be breached and that everyone will be faced with issues that cause profound and disturbing conflicts. At the younger levels of middle school and high school, there are similar issues, which tend to take the form of rationalized "turning a blind eye" and a lack of supervision and common sense on the part of parents, with denial and grandiosity on the part of younger adolescents.

Many analysts and therapists end up at the same place by rigid and blanket application of the basic professional ethical tenet of confidentiality. This is not hard to do, as we all are likely to share, to varied extent, the values and ideals of our own society, and an unquestioning monolithic stance of absolute silence about an adolescent's material provides a wall at one's back.

Our approach is quite different. We build on our assumptions that the major developmental tasks for late-adolescents include the transformation and integration of their changing bodies, minds, and identities with a transformed relationship to adults, particularly parents. The utility of such transformation is that the young adult can continue to use his parents as a support and resource in the difficult lifelong task of personal growth from being a child to becoming a responsible, creative, loving, and fulfilled adult, able eventually to parent others. The aim is not separation or solipsistic self-sufficiency, but increasing mastery, responsibility, interdependency, and interrelatedness. Within this theoretical frame, the issue of confidentiality takes a proportionate place in the hierarchy of therapeutic and parental values.

As noted earlier, we differentiate between privacy, a given of mental life in humans that rests on respect for oneself and others as individuals, and secrecy, a motivated withholding that is often hostile and is used to control or avoid genuine contact with others. Confidentiality should be maintained in support of privacy and not as a reflexive collusion with secrecy. The goal is to make any secrecy a legitimate object of analytic scrutiny and understanding so that the patient and his parents can find their way to fruitful sharing and communication of whatever is important to each and all of them. The analyst's task is to support these goals by respecting the privacy of thoughts and feelings in all the multiple alliances while examining actions with the patient and parents in their respective arenas of work together.

In line with our dual goals for any treatment, which comprise restoring the child to the path of progressive development and restoring the parent-child relationship to open-system transformative capacity, we see ongoing support for parents' primary responsibility for their child as one critical aspect of parent work. We work hard in the initial phases to place the parents in their rightful central position in the mental and emotional life of the child, and the child or adolescent in the center of the parents' consolidation in the phase of parenthood. Secrecy between parents and children is inimical to these aims. There are many experiences, thoughts, and feelings in the lives of parents and children that are private and therefore not each other's business, but the presence of secrets usually indicates the operation of pathological defenses or ways of relating that are very salient to the work of treatment. Parents who "don't want to know" are defensively abdicating their rightful role, often by externalizing responsibility onto the therapist to deal with unpleasant or painful issues in the child. We can describe our techniques for dealing with secrets in general terms as keeping safety and responsibility in the hands of parents, where they belong, even if this takes a long time to establish or reestablish throughout a treatment.

In practice, there are many technical ways to implement our assumptions. The most basic is simply to keep in mind that we are working toward parental assumption of appropriate responsibility. When we become aware, often through the revelation of a secret by a child or adolescent, that parents and children are out of touch with each other, our consciousness is raised to listen for opportunities to address the defensive externalization of ego functions. At other times, dangerous actions or planned actions by an adolescent demand direct intervention in the form of discussion with the patient about how he or she is going to enlist needed assistance or support from parents or other adults. The following are some examples of what we might actually say to patients or parents in various situations. These by no means exhaust the possibilities, but we hope they convey the sense that confidentiality is not a fixed attitude that takes over all other clinical values, but rather it contributes to safety and comfort for all parties in the therapeutic situation as a dynamic dimension of joint investigation.

> Twelve-year-old Nathan talked in his sessions about his excitement in setting fires. He and his friends used butane candle lighters to scorch various materials. The sexual excitement represented in this behavior was explored in treatment, and the analyst also raised the question of safety for Nathan and the house, asking if Nathan was being a good parent to himself by keeping everything safe enough. Nathan began to think through how to make it safer, but this material also alerted the analyst to a possible lack of parental vigilance. The parents were still seeing Nathan as a little boy rather than as a pubertal adolescent. Keeping in mind the hierarchy of clinical values that puts safety at the top of the list, the analyst began to listen closely in parent sessions for an opportunity to address the issue of parental disengagement from Nathan.
>
> In a parent session, this issue arose first in relation to the parents having no qualms about Nathan babysitting for a neighbor's little girl. Babysitting represented in part a progressive impulse for Nathan, in that he was seeking responsibility and earning capacity for the first time, but neither the boy nor the parents allowed themselves to think of any potential pitfalls. The therapist asked them what they thought of a pubertal boy caring intimately for a four-year-old girl. This allowed for a discussion of general difficulties in impulse control at Nathan's age and the continuing need for parental involvement and monitoring of activities to support the development of appropriate controls. The mother then remembered her thirteen-year-old cousin approaching her inappropriately during a family vacation and her parents intervening. The result of this work was a greater recognition on the part of the parents for Nathan as who he presently was—a person with growing strengths *and* continuing needs for his parents.

In this instance the analyst did not have to address with the parents the specific behavior of fire setting described in Nathan's sessions, but could address more importantly the general issue of impulsivity and Nathan's ongoing need for supportive supervision. This was an important shared experience for the therapist and the parents that was put to good use later in the treatment when Nathan briefly stole and shoplifted.

Sometimes parents call a therapist when they know something is wrong but struggle to allow themselves the full knowledge of their child's distress or the full seriousness of the situation. Their stance may not represent pathological denial but rather seems to be a less profound self-protective avoidance or hope that the therapist may tell them not to worry. The analyst's verbalization may be all that is needed to lead to a shared reality perception.

> The mother of fourteen-year-old Joanna phoned to ask if the therapist had a vacancy to treat her daughter who seemed to be increasingly unhappy. During the half-hour phone conversation, material emerged that sounded suicidal. The therapist asked the mother if she had any sense of her daughter's suicide plans. Although it had been the mother describing Joanna's miserable withdrawal, her giving away clothes to all her friends, her preoccupation with discussions of the afterlife, and so forth, the mother was shocked and surprised at the therapist's urgent concern. She exclaimed that Joanna had been a model child until recently, a deeply religious young person who could surely never contemplate behavior so sinful as suicide. She had felt that she shouldn't intrude on her daughter's moods, as she wanted to give her space to be a regular teenager.
> The therapist suggested that the mother talk with Joanna, sharing the concern, now articulated explicitly by their discussion, that she was thinking of harming herself. The mother was advised to work out with Joanna how she would keep a close eye on her while arranging a therapeutic evaluation for Joanna and her parents in order to address the situation.

In this instance, the therapist and the mother collaborated to come to initial joint understanding of the seriousness of Joanna's difficulties, and the mother was supported in taking responsibility for seeking help for her daughter.

Work with adolescents brings with it many instances that are not so straightforward where the therapist has to make difficult judgments about the degree of danger and the status of parental defenses. Overreaction can be damaging to the treatment relationships, but rigid adherence to the ideal of confidentiality may collude with parental denial and allow for a situation of extreme danger.

> Jake was a high-school senior preparing to leave for a prestigious university, his father's alma mater. He was in turmoil, determined to leave

but clearly unready to do so. His parents took it for granted that Jake would follow in the family tradition and wanted treatment to help him "pull himself together and get on with his life." As the work proceeded it became apparent to Jake and the analyst that removal of the obstacles to his further development would require much more than self-control and immediate effort. When Jake and the analyst met together with his parents to discuss this, the parents expressed concern and support, but at home they told Jake they were profoundly disappointed in him and expected him to try harder.

Jake was hurt and angry but shifted his rage to his girlfriend, whom he had encouraged to go out with another boy, and to his analyst, whom he characterized as "a stereotypical Jew only interested in money and taking advantage of helpless people like the Palestinians." He raged for weeks, broke up with his girlfriend, and began hinting at thoughts of killing himself. The analyst noted this, asking if Jake was planning to kill himself, perhaps to punish his girlfriend and his analyst. Jake said he had been having the thought of using one of his father's guns to blow his brains out against the windows at the entrance to the analyst's office "so everyone will see how terrible and useless you are!"

The analyst felt that Jake had an active suicide plan and was especially concerned when Jake mentioned using his father's gun. He told Jake that he thought he was in danger of killing himself and asked what could be done to help him stay alive. Did his parents know that he was suicidal? "Hell no," Jake shouted, "and if you tell them I'll have you sued for breaking confidentiality. You promised me that everything I say is confidential. So now you're a liar too!"

The analyst reminded Jake (and himself) that the initial discussions had stipulated that all Jake's thoughts and feelings were private, but that actions that posed a threat to his safety or to others took precedence; everyone was then responsible for ensuring his safety. He suggested that Jake start by telling him about father's guns and if he had access to them. Jake's anger subsided, and he told the analyst relatively calmly that his father was a gun collector, with everything from modern assault rifles to flintlocks from the eighteenth century. Most of the guns, especially the historical weapons, were kept in a locked display case, but Jake knew where the key was, and besides, he had recently noticed that there were always other guns lying around. "Is this a message?" Jake wondered, and then agreed that he needed help and that his parents should know his current suicidal state. He said he would speak with them right after the session. The therapist said he would call Jake in a couple of hours to hear how it had gone and what was happening.

On the phone Jake said that his parents seemed to be avoiding him, breaking off the conversation when he said he needed to have a serious talk with them. He was relieved when the analyst suggested a joint emergency meeting for that evening, at which Jake could tell his parents of his unbearable stress, his wish to please them, and his helplessness to do so. His hurt and anger and wish to kill himself felt like his only way out of the situation. His plan was to do it with one of his father's guns, so he needed his parents to take responsibility for suicide proofing the house.

At the meeting, which the parents attended only under pressure from the analyst, they first said that Jake was not serious, that he was being dramatic to manipulate the analyst and them in order to avoid his responsibilities. The therapist stated that he felt otherwise, that he was convinced that Jake would kill himself if his parents did not listen and take the danger seriously. They could demonstrate that they believed him by locking up the guns, keeping the ammunition in a separate place, and putting the keys to the gun case in their safe. The analyst said that he was inserting a note that day into Jake's file, noting the danger of suicide and that the need to seal off access to the guns had been discussed with Jake's parents.

The parents were taken aback, then agreed to lock up the guns as suggested. The analyst privately thought they were motivated as much by potential social embarrassment as by genuine concern for Jake, but their actions were critical to protecting Jake. A few weeks later, they gave indications of greater investment as parents when they said to Jake that they realized that his attending a particular college was not as important as his survival. As his treatment progressed, Jake and his parents became closer and more loving than at any time earlier in his adolescence.

The model of working with parents of children and adolescents in treatment that we are suggesting is not prescriptive. We are not replacing a prohibition against such work with a demand that all treatments of children and adolescents must include parent work to be effective. We work with what people bring, what they are capable of, what they can tolerate. We take them where they are—sometimes adolescents refuse to allow us to see their parents regularly or even to meet them. Adolescents and their parents have internalized the Anglo-American and psychoanalytic view that successful adolescent development means physical separation; having and keeping secrets is a means, endorsed by teenagers and their parents alike, to facilitate separation. They believe that any genuine communication between parent and child or therapist and parents threatens the developmental thrust and may lead to a regressive inability to separate.

As we discussed earlier, we see the goal of adolescent development as transformation. Transformation benefits from privacy, but secrecy can be used to avoid real change. In earlier work we have emphasized that adolescence provides a crucial opportunity to consolidate open-system functioning and set aside a closed-system, omnipotent relation to the self, others, and the world at large. With this in mind, we consider the issues of parent work and privacy/secrecy as central even if the parents are never seen.

> Kent's mother called to arrange therapy for her son and wanted to know if the analyst had a treatment vacancy. She did not want to discuss his difficulties, as that would be his job, and neither she nor her husband saw any reason to meet the therapist.
>
> Kent was a bright, charming sixteen-year-old who was a talented musician, taking college courses before graduating from high school and applying to excellent universities both in the United States and abroad. He had a long, steady relationship with a girl, which had recently become fully sexual. He did not abuse drugs or alcohol, had a few close friends, and claimed a good relationship with his parents. It wasn't clear quite why he wanted therapy, as there did not seem to be any major difficulties or interferences. However, when the therapist said he would like to meet Kent's parents, there was an emphatic refusal. Kent agreed to fill out the developmental history form with his parents, but he kept delaying and never did complete it or return the form to the analyst. He insisted on keeping his therapy totally walled off from his parents. The therapist agreed to go along with this for the time being, but noted this adamancy as something to explore further.
>
> Initially Kent used his sessions to consolidate his competent functioning and experience pleasure in being effective. Within the safety of consolidated open-system functioning, he began to experience an internal conflict between two ways of being—he acknowledged a pull to what he called "a state of passivity." In this state he watched videos, played video games, and watched pornographic movies. He reluctantly admitted to being "addicted" to pornographic Web sites, especially those with a sadomasochistic emphasis. Kent became anxious, wanting to know if this meant he was a pervert. He spoke of his delight at the sadistic power

he wielded with his younger sister and the other kids in middle school. Then in high school he began to feel bad for being so mean. He began to withdraw, to become passive, to keep his "power" to his fantasies.

Kent then spoke of the special closeness he had to his mother and of his disdain for his father. The analyst verbalized and Kent confirmed that he had conscious sexual daydreams about his mother and believed she would prefer him sexually to his father. The analyst then realized why Kent had to keep his analysis secret from his parents. It was not primarily shame or fear of retribution, but a fear of testing against reality his omnipotent belief that he could force his mother to meet all his needs, including sexual ones. Secrecy was in the service of protecting and retaining his belief in his omnipotence.

Later in the treatment, after a long period of work on Kent's various omnipotent beliefs, the analyst could engage him in thinking about the reality that if his mother truly loved him, as she seemed to, she would not have sex with him as she would realize how destructive this would be. Kent seemed to respond with relief. The year of analysis before he left for college appeared to benefit him greatly in general. The analyst, however, felt dissatisfied with the overall outcome as he felt that Kent's insistence on secrecy in order to retain a sense of omnipotence deprived Kent of a realistic lifelong resource of parental love.

Many adolescent treatments, as we noted above, fall short of an ideal structure including regular parent work, but the therapist's keeping in mind the tasks of parent work allows for accomplishment by various means.

Kitty was adamant that the therapist not meet with her mother in any regular way, as she assumed the therapist would crumble under the force of her mother's bossy and intrusive personality, just as Kitty felt herself doing when her mother asked daily what she had talked about in sessions. None of the therapist's assurances of being able to handle the situation, nor her interpretations of Kitty's attribution of omnipotent power to her mother, availed, so treatment was begun without a firm arrangement for communication between the parents and the therapist.

Kitty's mother telephoned the therapist with long, furious tirades of abuse against Kitty whenever they had one of their periodic hysterical arguments. The analyst consistently reminded her that she would tell Kitty they had talked, but listened and tried to help the mother see more clearly what her own and Kitty's experience in the fight might be. With

Kitty, the therapist used the mother's calls to look together at all sides of the issues represented in the fights and at how Kitty had tried to hold on to the battling style of relating so as to feel she had some power in her interactions with her mother. Over time, the wild disputes calmed down, and there were fewer urgent phone calls from Kitty's mother. As Kitty grew more in charge of her own feelings, her mother telephoned occasionally to report that Kitty had told her how important the treatment was to her and to say how happy she was to see Kitty progressing, growing up so well after the difficult times.

By accepting Kitty's treatment plan but reserving the ability to be available to the parents, who had their own needs, the analyst was able to stay equidistant from all parties and give the parents support for their healthier parenting, while analyzing Kitty's use of control in her relationships to both parents and therapist.

CHAPTER SEVEN

THE PRETERMINATION
PHASE OF TREATMENT

W e think it is important to define a pretermination phase of treatment in which both patient and analyst can explore whether
they are ready to enter into and make maximum use of the termination period (J. Novick and K. K. Novick 1996b; K. K. Novick and J.
Novick 1998). This phase of treatment is seldom discussed in the professional literature and is not discussed at all in relation to parents. The work
of pretermination has its own specific features, tasks, anxieties, and conflicts
for all parties.

> Luke's treatment moved quickly, with visible effects outside. He carved
> out a very lucrative, unique, and creative career that used his full intel-
> lectual capacities. He started a new relationship on the basis of thinking
> about the long term, rather than just the need to prove himself attrac-
> tive. He seemed to understand and relate to his mother in a different
> way, one that encompassed the complexity of his personality, their inter-
> action, and their history. He had earlier dropped out of college, partly
> because of his inability to finish anything, but he arranged to complete
> his studies. Both Luke and the analyst began to think about his finish-
> ing treatment.

Markers of Pretermination

Criteria for starting a termination phase differ significantly from the criteria used at the end of treatment to assess the relative success of the work

(J. Novick 1982, 1990; J. Novick and K. K. Novick 2002b). The patient, the analyst, or the parents, or any combination of the parties to the treatment, begin to think that an ending might be possible. Making the judgment tends initially to be felt, rather than thought through. Criteria may be based on a sense of movement or momentum, that is, a sense that progressive development is reinstated. We note an increase in pleasure, joy, creativity, and independent use of capacities, all hallmarks of open-system functioning. These criteria all hark back, however, to the explicit discussion during evaluation of how to know when treatment will be done. Therapists can remind parents of what they have been looking for all along and support the shared perception of a consolidation of progressive development.

Without setting a date, the analyst and patient discuss what will be involved, with the analyst describing in general terms how this part of the work can be structured and what can be accomplished. The analyst emphasizes the termination period as one of hard work that can bring great benefits. It is a time of consolidating therapeutic gains and internalizing the accomplishment of the therapeutic alliance tasks in the context of saying good-bye. This description prompts a joint assessment of work accomplished, work remaining, and a catalogue of capacities that will be called upon to do the work of termination.

Just the mention of termination often brings powerful reactions. The roots of these contain the potential for premature termination, forced by either patient or analyst, in the service of defensive avoidance on either side of renewed separation issues. The risk of ruining a good treatment is very high at this point.

Parent Work during Pretermination

But what about parents? In the conventional structure of parent work, parents have often been seen infrequently during the middle phase, and then they demand ending of treatment just at the point when pretermination ought to be initiated by patient and analyst. In such situations parents are anticipating an ending and seizing control of the process. Just when the parental task is to enjoy and validate their child's progression, they may be affected anew by fear of abandonment or a sense that they will now lack value or purpose. They may feel useless and unloved and as well may suffer a transference fear of being discarded and rejected by the analyst.

A preemptive, premature termination forced by parents at this point can represent a passive-to-active defense that leaves the therapist the one feeling useless and abandoned. Analysts may defend against their own hurt and anger in such a situation by rationalizing the end as a normal aspect of child development, especially of adolescent development. Here it is useful to call upon the concept of a pretermination phase and to explain its importance to parents so that they can again be enlisted to work together toward a planned termination phase.

Regular work with parents throughout the treatment usually prevents a preemptive strike and a premature termination. Indeed we have often experienced a different response. Some parents, when told that ending is on the horizon, say, "Don't rush it" or "Don't rock the boat when everything is going so smoothly."

> Luke's parents were relieved and pleased with their new level of relationship with him. His mother was seldom so intensely angry at him, and father and son were sharing many interests, frequently supporting each other in their separate endeavors. When it was discussed in a parent session that it seemed that Luke was moving into a pretermination phase, his mother expressed concern about rushing things. His father said to the analyst, "I know you have been seeing him for a long time, and you must be getting bored or impatient, but do you think it's wise to end before we are sure there won't be a relapse?"

The first task for the analyst was to help them with their anxiety that without treatment and the analyst Luke would revert to his suicidal, sado-masochistic functioning. They lacked confidence that he and they could independently sustain a loving relationship.

At this point Luke was twenty-one, chronologically an adult, but his parents still paid a large proportion of the cost of his treatment. Most child analysts, trained as we also were, tend to stay at arm's length from the parents of their adolescent patients. Work with Luke and other young adults has led us to reconsider this position, and we now routinely find ways to work with the parents of adolescents.

During the early years of Luke's analysis, Luke had participated in the weekly parent sessions, but he soon realized that the focus was on their parenting skills. As the parent work had deepened and turned to the parents' own conflicts about being good parents, Luke felt that his presence was inhibiting their work. He knew that his individual work was private but that the analyst would share with him aspects of the parent work if it seemed it would be helpful to his growth. Further, Luke and his parents knew that joint meetings were possible whenever they wanted.

In the middle phase of Luke's treatment, his parents kept contact with the analyst and conducted their work by phone, e-mail, and monthly meetings. Periodically Luke asked about the goals of the parent work, as he realized that his parents' specific goals changed as he changed. Luke helped to articulate his parents' tasks for each phase of his treatment.

As Luke's pretermination work intensified, he suggested to the analyst that he thought his parents needed to be seen more often again, as he thought they felt unready to have him finish his treatment. He was picking up their difficulty in the pretermination parent task of, in Furman's words, "standing by to admire" (E. Furman 1992, 119). This demands of the parents (and of the analyst) that they forgo the intense gratification of earlier steps of "doing for" and "doing with" the child in favor of meeting the child's need to have the parents and other important people take pleasure in his feelings of mastery and achievements, appreciate his creativity and accomplishments, trust him and encourage him in moments of frustration, and allow him to develop confidence in himself.

Luke's parents struggled with their old propensity to fear Luke's skills and competence as destructive and hostile, thus confirming his omnipotent belief in his destructiveness. In "standing by to admire," they were recognizing and respecting his separate positive capacities. But they were also allowing him to experience his pathological omnipotent sadomasochistic beliefs as his own construction, which he alone could choose to set aside or retain.

The analyst first took up Luke's parents' anxiety by affirming that nothing would be decided until they could explore the reasons for their concern. Their most conscious worry was that the end would come upon them quickly, without careful consideration. Although the perceptions informed the analyst's thinking, the analyst did not enter into what, by then, was their familiar obsessionality, their inability to make decisions about anything, and their counterreactive impulsivity, followed by years of regret. Rather, the analyst stayed on the level of providing a general explanation of how treatments of long duration end and the importance of the termination period for consolidating the positive gains. The pretermination period was described as the time for assessing readiness for the work of a termination period.

This provided immediate reassurance, which allowed the analyst to then shift the focus to the parents' tasks during this phase, with the idea that they could work to consolidate the gains they had made in their parenting. An immediate difficulty arose, as Luke's mother continued to resist any work that might threaten her defensive position of blamelessness for any of Luke's past difficulties. She continued to feel that he had been a monster; she thought that the positive change in their relationship was a result of his "at last coming to his senses" and deciding at least to act in a civilized manner. She appreciated the work Luke had done in therapy, but found little value in the parent work. She was relieved that there would not be a precipitate ending and hoped there would be no reversion to his "throwing fits" as soon as treatment ended.

Parents and analyst decided that father would continue to attend parent sessions regularly and convey important things to mother. The door was left open for her attendance at any time. In the next session, alone, Luke's father talked about his sense that his wife could not manage any threat to her externalizing, blaming style. He noted that he now protects Luke and accepts that at times he has to "serve as the bad guy. That's the way she is, and she won't change. There always has to be some bad man out there to blame." Work focused on the realignment in the family, with father taking an active role in realistic rescue and protection of the children from the abusive mother.

Father e-mailed his insight that one of his worries about the end of Luke's treatment was that he would "be out of a job. If Luke doesn't need to stay in treatment, if he can take care of himself, then he doesn't need me to protect him, and then what's left? Wow! I have to keep him a helpless child so that I can be a valued father. What a crock of shit! Luke and I have so much more going for us. I realized that my anxiety about his mother was really an anxiety about the end of my usefulness. What else is there? See you next week."

Before the next meeting, father wrote, "There is more—my envy. How I wish that I could have had analysis at his age. Perhaps I could have been as happy and creative and productive as he is. Isn't it strange to envy my own son even when he is benefiting from what I have provided for him? What next? See you Tuesday."

Next was father's awareness of how angry he felt with his own father, who had been the passive bystander while his wife (Luke's grandmother) controlled and abused the children. He was angry and sad during the session. He said, "I don't know how many generations of the men in my family carried on the pattern of marrying powerful, controlling, abusive women and stood by as their own children were destroyed. I've been in my own therapy for years. I've been helped in many ways. I'm very grateful, but it's only in our work together on my parenting that I could see and feel this repeated pattern of allowing our sons to be abused. I hope that it's not too late to stop this. I hope the change in my relationship with Luke can provide him with a different model of how a father can be." He then wondered if he could get enough done before Luke finished treatment.

The therapist said that they would work until the end, but if necessary they could continue working on parent issues after Luke's work ended. Father seemed pleased that he wasn't working under a time constraint, but then cancelled the next session, claiming pressing business needs. That evening he e-mailed, "I'm sure you didn't believe the bullshit about work. I did have urgent matters, but I always do. I had convinced myself that I couldn't spare the time. I first realized that I couldn't bear the thought of Luke surpassing me—being more successful, happier, and nicer than I am. But then it struck me that I am talking about my surpassing my father. This is an issue I've worked on in my own therapy, but never in terms of my being a better father. For years I've worked on my guilt for surpassing my father physically, sexually, academically, and financially. This must be the last battle. A part of me wants to be as bad a father as my dad was with me. Can we meet an extra time this next week?"

At the next few meetings, Luke's father spoke of his enjoyment spending time with his son. "It is like having a fascinating friend. I love to listen to him talk about his work and his life. I don't mind when I have little to add. It's just wonderful to listen to him. I feel so proud of him. His new venture is filled with risks, but I'm confident he'll make it work."

Soon after, Luke cleared the last hurdle of the pretermination phase. He felt ready and confident to start a time of saying good-bye. In the next week he chose a date three months ahead for finishing his analysis, and the termination period could begin.

This intensive period of work with Luke and his parents was crucial to the completion of his treatment and the restoration to progressive development of both the adolescent and his parents. Despite the handicap of their individual histories, Luke's parents each entered into the work to their fullest capacity. His mother was unable to bear working directly, but she tolerated and appreciated the changes in the other family members over time. To the extent she was able, she made use indirectly of the insights achieved in the parent work. Luke's father made crucial leaps forward in his own therapy under the impetus of the parent work and was able to bring these gains into his personal life and his parenting, to Luke's great benefit.

From the analyst's point of view, the technical issues in the pretermination phase with Luke's parents involved letting each of them, particularly father, work as independently as they could, while providing support and "standing by to admire" them as well. What is important to underline here, however, is how active this stance is, how work with parents continues to be important and intense even in the closing stages of treatment, and even in work with adolescents and young adults.

The transition between the pretermination and termination phases is marked by agreement among child, analyst, and parents on a date for ending. After setting the date, child and parents enter with the analyst into the work of the termination phase.

THE TERMINATION PHASE OF TREATMENT

D espite a spate of papers in the last thirty years on the topic of termination, the ending of treatment for adults and children remains an area of difficulty and conceptual controversy. This
seems especially true in regard to termination work with parents. All too
frequently, children and adolescents end treatment prematurely because of
a unilateral decision on the part of their parents (J. Novick 1990). Our
present focus on parent work derives from our experience that it is essential to a genuine completion of a child analysis that parents be an explicit
part of the treatment plan throughout. Earlier chapters have detailed conflicts, anxieties, and resistances that arise in parents and have suggested
techniques for addressing them at each phase of treatment. Here we will
look at issues in the termination phase.

Termination of Parent Work

Assuming that there has been consistent work with parents throughout
treatment, patient, parents, and analyst enter the termination phase with
an agreed-upon ending date and a shared understanding of the tasks remaining to be accomplished. For the first time in the treatment, there is
relatively little danger of a premature, unilateral termination. But termination work with parents is crucial to helping them to support their child's
adaptive use of the termination work; to meet the child's legitimate need
for a supportive, validating person when the analyst is no longer available;

and to foster their own autonomous capacity to use the positive parenting skills they have developed. Another way to describe the task of parents during the termination phase is in terms of consolidation of the open-system functioning they have been able to achieve through the work of mastering the therapeutic alliance tasks of each phase of the treatment. The therapeutic alliance tasks for parents during termination are to allow the child and themselves to mourn and thus internalize their own relationship with the analyst in order to be able to carry on their parental development after treatment.

These are significant demands on parents, which can give rise to fears of sadness, love, and loss, and to fears of reliving core experiences of grief and conflict around good-byes. Parents may try to deal with these anxieties by avoidance or premature withdrawal from the parent work, or they may use parent work as an opportunity to learn a new way of saying good-bye.

Reality of the Relationship between Parents and Therapist

It is important for the analyst to acknowledge internally and explicitly that the parents and the therapist have a deep and significant bond. Saying good-bye to each other will inevitably evoke the complex feelings, anxieties, and defenses associated with separation and loss. This is true even if the parents and analyst have never actually met—for instance, when a late-adolescent has been in treatment during college attendance far from home. But they have all been part of an important effort together in the service of the patient's development, and this creates a strong attachment. We say to parents that we adults need a good-bye time just as much as the child does; this is often particularly true for single parents, who may have used the relationship with the child's therapist for critical support in their parental functioning.

Ordinary Parental Anxieties during Termination

At this time we listen for, and introduce if they are not forthcoming, parents' questions about posttherapy contact. We try to detoxify the issue—that is, counteract any remaining idea of a relationship maintained by pain or pathology—by talking about their capacity to continue the work begun together through the therapy, about how they now have the skills inside because they have learned to listen differently and enlist their child in understanding and growing. We take up the magical, omnipotent belief that life can be trouble free, and that therefore treatment should ensure a smooth passage, by introducing the idea that what they and their child have developed in treatment is "emotional muscle," a tolerance for ordinary stresses and strains. We also think through together how they will know if they have reached an impasse or have become stuck in trying to work on a problem. Here we point out that parents and analyst will always have a relationship, that the analyst is a lifelong resource. By exploring their feelings around potential future contact, remnants of guilt and shame may once more be addressed and the feeling of teamwork reinforced.

Resistance to Love and Sadness

Just as the termination phase allows for a final reworking of core conflicts for the individual patient, so parents, faced with the reality of ending, often react with their characteristic anxieties and defenses. This was what we saw in the case of Tamara, who started a termination phase at twelve, after two and a half years of analysis.

> Throughout Tamara's treatment her parents had difficulty in allowing her psychological autonomy. This stemmed from intense anxiety about the power of Tamara's feelings, especially her anger and rejection of her parents, which in turn was based on a pathological belief in the omnipotence of feelings. The rigid suppression and control they had exercised to deal with this had largely disappeared by the time the decision to terminate was made jointly by child, parents, and analyst.
>
> As soon as the date was set, however, Tamara's mother became angry and depressed, like at the beginning of the treatment, and Tamara's father again seemed helpless and discouraged, ineffectual in dealing with his own anger at his daughter and his wife. At the same time, some of the life seemed to go out of Tamara in her sessions. The analyst noted the similarity of this pattern to the beginning of the analysis and talked with the parents about all the changes that had taken place. In describing the hard work they had all done, the analyst remarked on how much they had gone through together, and how close this had made them all

feel. Father then exclaimed, "Yes, it will really feel strange not to be coming here anymore." Mother sighed and frowned and said that it would be a relief, as then she could take Tamara to gymnastics. In the next week, mother continued to talk enthusiastically with Tamara about how much fun it was going to be when treatment ended. Both parents were struggling with their own conflicts about feelings, pushing away their good feelings about the analyst and the treatment for fear of sadness. But this also meant that they would then be unable to mourn their own loss; internalize the gains; and, importantly, to absorb, tolerate, and support Tamara's mourning.

The mother's reaction related to a central issue in her character and a lifelong anxiety that her child would hate her. The analyst returned to the mother's shame at the impact of her rage and depression on her child and the humiliation of having a child in treatment—long-standing themes in the parent work throughout. Tamara's mother cried as she described how much happier and more loving her daughter had become and how bad she felt that her daughter had been so unhappy before the treatment. Here in the termination phase was the need for continuing work on the transformation of guilt into usable concern that was begun at the evaluation. In the termination phase, some parents still struggle with achieving remorse that allows for reparation. The analyst addressed the magical assumption contained in the mother's guilt—that she should somehow be able to change the past—and suggested that mother focus on the tools she now had available to ensure that the future was different from the past.

At the same time, Tamara's father grappled with his defensive inhibition of feelings. When the analyst greeted his comment about how it would be when they didn't meet anymore with the acknowledgment, "Yes we will miss each other," father was able to own his good feelings for the work. He talked about how he and his wife had grown along with their daughter and began to perceive the intensity of Tamara's feelings about the end of her treatment. When the analyst remarked that they might consider sharing their perceptions and feelings with their daughter, both parents smiled and said, "That will help us all!"

Tamara's parents needed to work during the termination period to tolerate their child's sadness and to acknowledge their own. Mourning is only possible when there are loving feelings, and internalization does not take place without mourning—hence the critical importance of a good termi-

144

nation to the consolidation of therapeutic work and the parents' capacity to continue growing and fostering their child's growth subsequently.

Reworking of Core Conflicts and Generational Issues during Termination

In previous chapters, we have followed the course of parent work in conjunction with the treatment of Luke, the twenty-two-year-old who had started treatment at sixteen after nearly dying from a suicide attempt.

At the start of his analysis Luke, like his father, had a very limited range of emotional experience or expression. Through the generations, the men in his family took pride in their ability to withstand harrowing physical or psychological assault without displaying any feeling. Luke had outbursts of rage or moments of sadistic glee when he bested an opponent. Any other feeling, such as love, sadness, or sympathy, was considered counterproductive and a sign of weakness.

By the end of treatment both father and son had an alternative to the family ideal of macho mercenary men kept in check only by domineering women. Luke came to this sooner and more extensively; he also had greater certainty that being a loving, caring, feeling man was preferable to being a sadistic, cold, emotionally dead person. During the course of the parent work, Luke's father had also extended his range of feelings, but this new way of being was limited to his relationship with his son. Given father's own history of multiple losses and separations, it was not surprising that he reacted to the termination decision with his longstanding character armor of emotional withdrawal.

Luke's father was cordial and distracted in parent sessions as the fourteen-week countdown to termination began. He no longer seemed to feel any concern about Luke's capacity to maintain his positive changes. In a turnaround from his earlier worry that it might be rushing things to consider termination, once the date was set he wondered if a three-month ending period was needlessly prolonging the good-bye. "As far as I'm concerned, there's nothing more to work on. I won't interfere with your work with Luke, but our work on my parenting issues and my relationship with my son seems to have reached an end. My son and I are getting along well—we enjoy and respect each other. I'm glad. I'm grateful. But I think we can stop now."

The analyst agreed that father and son had come a long way, but pointed out that termination is a time of consolidation. Luke was doing that in his treatment, and it might be helpful to father to do the same, to go over what they had learned together and thus ensure that the positive changes could become a permanent part of father's personality. Luke's father saw the logic in that and agreed to continue through Luke's termination phase.

The analyst focused mainly on the changes in the range of father's feelings toward Luke, how father could now experience and express love, sadness, remorse, and worry. In the context of the family tradition of toughness, such changes were even more impressive and remarkable, a praiseworthy product of very hard work. Then the analyst spoke of Luke's struggle to extend this open-system way of relating to all his relationships, beyond those he considered safe, like those with his father and brother. Luke had discovered that he was far less vulnerable and more in realistic control if he let himself feel the full range of feelings in any relationship. He did this, the analyst said, by practicing in his therapy, allowing himself to know and express love, sadness, hurt, anger, disappointment, pride, and so forth. This allowed Luke to find pleasure at work and a meaningful relationship with both his parents.

Father added his perception of the change in Luke's dating pattern, in his making a more permanent relationship with a very nice person. "But," he said, "this is another area where Luke has gone beyond me. I don't think I ever loved anyone until my children were born, and then I didn't know how to love them. Here, with you, I've learned that it's good to be able to feel and express my love for them. But I'm the same cold, unfeeling prick with everyone else, including my wife."

The analyst took up this perception, noting that it was a considerable achievement to be able to tolerate and enjoy differences in skills, styles of thinking, accomplishments, and so forth. However, differences in self-protective emotional stances often create tensions in relationships. Without realizing it consciously, Luke and his father might each feel threatened by their different ways of dealing with feelings, and that could naturally lead to retreating from each other. Father wondered what to do about it. The analyst suggested that father, like Luke, could practice these skills in the safe setting of the parent work relationship, with the current task of saying good-bye. As this was the end of a very long and important relationship, perhaps he could allow himself to feel and express his feelings. As tears came to the father's eyes, the analyst added that this was indeed a meaningful relationship for them both, and that Luke and his father would be very much missed.

Luke's father associated to his own memory of his father's departure for wartime service when he was three years old. He had cried, and his parents told him that he was a little soldier and that brave soldiers don't cry, that if he had to cry like a little baby he should go to his room. He recalled taking deep breaths, telling himself not to cry and then feeling very grown up and proud when praised by his parents. His father was killed a year later, and again he felt proud for not crying, for being a brave little soldier.

Luke's mother had dropped out of the direct parent work during the middle phase of Luke's analysis, as she had felt too threatened by the prospect of addressing her responsibility for Luke's abused childhood. She had, however, continued to work at a distance, making use of what her husband brought back from parent sessions and changing in her interactions with Luke. The analyst invited her to come back to parent sessions to say good-bye. She attended a couple of times and expressed her sense that the whole family had gained a tremendous amount from the years of work together. Parent work with Luke's mother had some impact, but the limitations were also clear, in that her character was constructed on the basis of externalizations that she could not relinquish.

In the last seven weeks of the termination period, in the context of his sadness at saying good-bye, Luke's father went over the positive changes in his parenting, especially his newfound capacity to respect and enjoy his son's separate existence. With his practice at feeling a fuller range of affects also came some negative feelings of disillusionment and disappointment in the analyst and the process. In particular, both Luke and his father had to come to terms with their feelings about the fact that what we have termed "closed-system sadomasochistic functioning" was still present and available. It had not been eradicated, only decreased in intensity and contained by alternative open-system possibilities. They would both have to continue working after analysis to address conflicts between these alternative ways to regulate themselves and resolve conflicts. But they were equipped with the capacities gained in the course of mastering the therapeutic alliance tasks during each phase of treatment. Father and Luke could then imagine the postanalytic phase realistically, sensitive to signs of reverting to closed-system functioning and aware of being equipped to deal with these conflicts. This included the knowledge that they could contact the analyst at any time if they needed or wanted to.

Transforming Vulnerabilities into Strengths

Each therapeutic alliance task highlights particular parental resistances, but also points to possibilities of positive transformations.

> In the course of Henry's analysis, his mother's separation anxiety also contained her loving wish to be close to Henry and to provide for his needs. Her omnipotent guilt could be transformed to realistic remorse; her fear of being discarded and abandoned could be palliated by a growing pleasure in Henry's autonomy and competence; and she could use the model of her child's increasing ability to internalize responsibility, to tolerate strong affects, and to say good-bye without disintegrating to help her relate to her child on new levels. Henry's father transformed his identification with Henry's pathology to an appreciation of the strengths they could share.

Separation Reactions in Parents

There are some parents who are not ready to finish the work with the therapist, who continue to struggle with the tasks of parenthood and especially of allowing the child a separate existence. This problem may appear in the form of reluctance to allow the child to finish and in apparently extreme anxiety about their own or the child's ability to cope without the therapist. When this difficulty has appeared during the pretermination phase, we sometimes delay the termination decision to allow parents time to catch up. If they have seemed to do well with the decision to terminate and the anxiety escalates only during termination, it may be an acute reaction to separation. Often, acknowledgment of the importance of the relationship and the sadness of ending, together with verbalization of the fearful belief that the end will be like death, is sufficient. Sometimes, however, extreme parental anxiety during the termination phase has different implications.

Severe Pathology in Parents: Continuing Parent Work

In the chapter on beginning the treatment we noted that the parents of child and adolescent patients that we see are often more disturbed than individual adults who seek treatment for themselves. Like Luke's mother they may deny all responsibility for any psychological problems. Blame and responsibility are externalized, and the idea of individual therapy is too threatening to even consider.

Some tolerate parent work throughout the child's treatment, apply what is worked on, and show great gains. But, as termination approaches, it becomes clear that they cannot internalize and consolidate what they have learned. It seems as if the parental ego and superego in these situations is dependent upon the presence of the analyst. Parents with these difficulties will not be able to support their children in maintaining the progressive momentum regained through analysis. In these cases we explore the possibility of continuing to work with the parents after the end of the child's treatment. Then we must work carefully with the child to discover his or her feelings about this; we describe that the work with the parents will not be about the child, but rather to help them with some of the difficulties they have as parents, none of which is unfamiliar to the child. When this structure is really needed, most children are relieved to know that their parents will have the therapist available. The realities and limitations of this relationship as a conduit from the child to the analyst are explored in relation to the child's various fantasies about continuing contact. Then we continue to see the parent or parents, with the additional goal of making a referral for individual treatment so that they can address the personality difficulties that hold them back from open-system functioning and growth as parents. Eventually they too will be able to internalize accomplishment of the therapeutic alliance tasks and finish that part of the parenting work that they have done with their child's analyst.

CHAPTER NINE
POSTTERMINATION

T
he time after finishing cannot strictly be considered a phase of treatment, yet all the preceding work has been aimed at enhancing later functioning in parents and children, and a specific goal of treatment has been to equip them to continue working and growing on their own. There is a growing literature on posttermination in individual treatments of adults, but very little about this phase in child and adolescent patients and nothing about parents. This is another juncture where we have found our conceptualization of phase-specific therapeutic alliance tasks useful, both in setting criteria for moving into a termination phase and in defining the goals. This leads in turn to understanding criteria and goals in relation to the time after treatment.

Tasks of Postanalytic Life

We talk with patients and their parents during the termination phase about the tasks of postanalytic living. In particular we focus on the inevitable disappointments of life; the necessity for continued work, internally and in their relationships; and the type of postanalytic contact appropriate to the continuing analytic relationship. Discussion during termination concerns how they will feel when they experience disillusionment and disappointment with the analyst and the analysis and what it will be like when they surpass the analyst's understanding in their independent work—we raise these issues for parents to think about so that they will not be surprised later. Then the gains of treatment are more likely to be maintained.

Varieties of Posttreatment Contacts with Parents

Despite the difficulties that can arise in cases of severe parental pathology, most parents are ready to finish work at the same time as their children. Indeed, this synchrony is one measure of the renewal of closeness at a new level in the parent-child relationship. There is a whole spectrum of ways that parents in our experience have used the opportunity of postanalytic contact. Sometimes we never hear from a family again after termination. These have usually been cases in which we have done a minimum of parent work.

Consulting the Analyst

When we have worked consistently with parents, one common pattern is to hear from parents when some big decision faces the family. It is not so much that they seek advice or help; rather it is a form of consultation, as with the parents of Felicia, a child who had been in therapy for unhappiness and somnambulism from ages eight to ten.

Felicia had worked very effectively to address her highly anxious, perfectionistic, and demanding relationship with herself and her parents. Her harsh internal standards had intersected with a number of untimely deaths in her immediate circle, which had exacerbated her troubles. Once in therapy, her symptoms abated, and she was eventually able to enjoy school and friends in new, dependable ways. Her parents had both faithfully attended parent sessions through which they came to develop greater insight into their little girl's ways of thinking and to respect her feelings, while retaining their parental authority. Everyone felt it had been a very successful treatment.

Eight months after termination, the parent of one of Felicia's classmates died suddenly. The parents called the analyst to talk about their handling of this news and their plans about funeral attendance and so forth. Their call was in the nature of "running it by the analyst." The analyst thought they had made very good use of their gains from treatment, making wise decisions and speaking sensitively and sensibly with

152

their daughter. These parents had learned how to think about what was meaningful to Felicia, how to stay with her, how to communicate, and how to value their importance in helping their daughter through the sometimes hard vagaries of life.

News

Occasionally a parent shows great empathy during the termination phase for the analyst's loss when treatment finishes. This seems to be due to the analyst having succeeded in reassuring the parents that they are indeed the most important people to the child and that the analyst is not in competition. These are parents who then feel they can securely share the child with the analyst, as we saw with Kyla's mother.

> Kyla started treatment as a violently aggressive preschooler and finished successfully at the age of seven. Much of the parent work addressed the parents' valuing of themselves and how to help their child with loyalty conflicts between their very different parenting styles.
>
> Several months after the end of therapy, Kyla's mother phoned the analyst "because I knew you would so appreciate this." She described coming home from work and snapping angrily at Kyla. Later she apologized and explained to the child in some detail about her sense that she was taking something out on Kyla that really belonged in another situation. Uncertain about whether this concept was getting across, she asked Kyla, only to be met with a big grin and the remark, "Of course I understand how people sometimes do that, why do you think I went to my analyst for so long?"

Negotiating Developmental Transitions

A potential difficulty for families is their child's passage from one developmental phase to the next. Throughout the work with parents, we try to anticipate the issues these transitions may bring in the future, noting parents' problematic reactions to phase changes during treatment and the meanings ascribed to them, often as losses or separations. We talk to parents about what to expect in latency or adolescence and about how to monitor their own reactions. Posttreatment contact is often initiated by parents at these moments, as we saw repeatedly in the case of Christina, who met with her therapist intermittently over fifteen years.

Christina's parents had divorced acrimoniously when she was a toddler, but had agreed on joint custody. The course of their arrangements never ran smoothly, but the different sets of parents/stepparents had each come to separate parent sessions throughout Christina's treatment during her preschool and early school years. In that work they had become able to function together as parents to put their child's needs above their own wish to beat each other.

Each time Christina entered a new phase, however, all four parents seemed to struggle to stay securely ensconced in the phase of parenthood. Old defensive patterns of relating with each other and with Christina flared up and interfered with Christina's progressive development. Christina found her parents impossibly demanding and rigid, and the parents were at loggerheads. Each time—at the entrance to middle school, to high school, and to college—Christina asked to see the analyst. After two sessions on each of these occasions, it became clear that Christina was doing well, maintaining her progressive development, but that it was threatened by her parents' conflicts. The analyst met jointly with Christina and all four parents to talk through the practical issues about which they were having such trouble. Although the sessions focused on discussing concrete problems like school choice or use of a car, the process and the presence of the analyst seemed to reestablish the parents in the phase of parenthood they had achieved earlier.

Return to Treatment

An important measure of the solidity and depth of parent work in a child or adolescent treatment is the parents' capacity to return without shame, guilt, or reproach to see the analyst when they are concerned that their child is running into difficulties. Sometimes a few sessions of parent work can resolve the worry if it springs from parental reaction to developmental shifts, as we saw from Christina's situation, or from disagreement between parents who simply need a setting in which to talk the issue through.

Sometimes, however, parents have accurately perceived that their child is foundering in the face of new challenges from development or outside circumstances. When the child or adolescent reenters treatment, the parent work can proceed on the foundation of the strong positive working relationship established in the first treatment. Parents and analyst know each other very well, and the work is efficient and deep at the same time.

Long-Term Follow-Up

One criterion for self-monitoring that we discuss with both patient and parents during the termination phase is the nature of the internal image they carry of the analyst after finishing.

> Jane had ended her analysis at twenty-one after five years of work on her suicidal impulses. Work with her parents ended at the same time. In the four or five years afterward, the analyst received occasional notes from Jane about important developments—her marriage, her first publication, the births of her children. There had been no news for twelve years when Jane called the analyst for an appointment, saying that she had fallen into a terrible, suicidal depression like before she began treatment. When she was feeling hopeless, her mother had reminded her of how the analyst had talked about monitoring her internal images. When Jane saw that she had lost her sense of the analyst as a benign, loving resource, she realized that she was killing off something important inside herself and that this was a real danger signal. Jane and her mother were able to use tools from the adolescent treatment to deal with a current adult crisis.

Work with parents can lead to a deep, unforgettable experience for all parties, as we saw with Jane's mother, who kept the image of Jane's analyst alive inside for her daughter even when Jane could not. A last example comes from the treatment of Robert, who began analysis at three, having no language and with a diagnosis of atypical or autistic development. He finished his treatment at seven years of age.

> Robert's treatment had ended thirty years earlier. The analyst had not heard from the family since. Robert's parents saw a notice of a conference at the center where he had been treated, with the analyst's name featured as a speaker. Robert's mother left the following letter: "The reason I wanted to write to you for so long was to say that things have turned out so well for Robert." She described his school career, with success in academics and with friends, and his constructive and explorative adolescence. "He loved university where he also met his future wife." She said he had done very well and had pursued a career as a professional. "He has plenty of work, is very good at it, and loves it. He is happily married with two children. He is an exceptionally gifted and good father, as well as an excellent cook! He stands six foot four inches,

is very serious and occasionally tense. He is very self-aware and totally honest about himself; he is affectionate and able to express his feelings. I think he is happy on the whole.

"I thought you'd like to know about him, because you made a great contribution to his development by encouraging him to come out of his confines.

"Lastly I wanted to say that I too benefited from my visits to see you during a pretty difficult period in my life. For all this many thanks."

THE APPLICATION OF OUR MODEL OF PARENT WORK TO INDIVIDUAL TREATMENT OF ADULTS

The Continuum of Development and of Technique

C hild analysts have often been hesitant to insist on the centrality of our developmental understanding to psychoanalysis as a whole. Work with children and adolescents, which optimally includes work with parents, can be a wellspring for greater understanding of the health and pathology of the parenting function within each of us and of each adult patient. In adult work we almost never deal with the real parents of the patient, and so it would appear that this aspect of child work does not apply to the treatment of adults. If, however, we assume some continuity between child and adult development, and therefore continuity between child and adult techniques, we must ask about the place of the parental alliance in the therapeutic alliance tasks of each phase of treatment with the individual adult patient.

Evaluation

Among the many possible ways to conceptualize the role of parents in the psychological life of adults, there are four that relate particularly to the therapeutic alliance. They can be assessed during the evaluation and beginning phases of treatment.

Internalization of Parental Functions

The first is the degree of internalization of parental functions such as bodily care and management; regulation and control of feelings and impulses; provision of affirmation, validation, love, and praise; setting goals and standards; and providing meaning and direction. In the course of development, these parental functions are internalized and also remain open to reinforcement or change by the influence of teachers, mentors, and peers. Analysts of adults can assess the internalization of parental functions and images in the superego and the ego ideal as both potential resistance to and motivation for the alliance.

Quality of Self-Regard and Love

A second parental dimension relates to the quality of self-regard and love. How does the adult patient love and value his body and mind? Is the love capricious, unrealistic, and infantile? How consistently does he pay attention to and take care of his body; does he feel he owns his body? At the evaluation stage, we take note of this dimension of internal parenting to assess the degree to which hate and depreciation of self might lead to sabotage of treatment and how much the patient's love and valuing of self may be called upon to motivate engagement in difficult and painful work. Just as we do in parent work, we may articulate for individual adult patients a treatment goal of transformations of dangerous inattentiveness to appropriate self-protection and care, from masochistic misuse of the body or mind for perverse defenses and gratifications to a realistic acceptance, ownership, and enjoyment.

Externalized Parent-Child Relationship Patterns

The third involves our looking to see who currently performs parental functions or plays parental roles for the patient and what kind of relationship the patient has with these parental figures. The situation is analogous to that with the child patient and his parent, but the therapist of the adult usually cannot deal directly with the significant other who is performing parental functions to some degree. Many child cases are lost through insufficient attention to the therapeutic alliance with parents. So too are many adult cases if the therapist does not address directly in the evaluation the impact on the patient of, for instance, the husband who begrudges payment for his wife's therapy, the friend or sibling who denigrates it, or the wife who feels threatened and jealous at the prospect of her husband's intense involvement with an analyst. If the adult patient has externalized parental functions onto such figures in his current environment, the transformation to becoming a patient, which must be effected during the evaluation, will involve a significant shift in his relationship with these important others. We must verbalize and acknowledge the intense feelings this generates in all parties as a beginning of work on transforming externalized parent-child patterns being lived out in current relationships into internally experienced conflicts to be understood in therapy.

Achievement of the Developmental Phase of Parenthood

The fourth way we apply what we have learned from work with parents of child patients to the evaluation of adults is to note how the adult patient functions as a parent, whether or not he has children. Can the patient care for, empathize with, and show concern for others, or does he have an externalizing, abusive relationship with others who are used for infantile gratification, defense, safety, self-definition, and survival? If the patient has children, it is often in the account of interactions with them that perverse relationships are highlighted. These problems can then be included in the elucidation of treatment goals, and the wish to improve relationships becomes a source of motivation for the formation of a therapeutic alliance.

Analysts experienced in working with parents of child and adolescent patients are generally alert to parenting issues in the treatment of individual adults. The wish to be a good parent can be enlisted in parent work; similarly, this deep feeling can serve as the best, sometimes the only, motivation to keep an adult in treatment.

> A young woman started analysis for depression and panic attacks soon after her marriage to a highly successful, controlling man, toward whom she repeated her outwardly compliant relationship with her father. After a year of work, she could manage her rage in a more adaptive way, had overcome her depression and panic, and had made significant strides toward a more adult view of her relationship with her husband. She became pregnant, and both she and her husband thought that treatment should soon end, citing time and money issues. This coincided with both

his increasingly explicit annoyance at his wife's decrease in docility and her mixed feelings as the analytic work began to undermine her idealization of her parents.

As her pregnancy proceeded past the initial physical reactions, excitement, and anxiety of the first trimester, she began to imagine being a parent. For the first time she was openly critical of how her parents had dealt with her and her siblings when she was a child. She was in conflict, as she didn't want to repeat what she currently saw as major defects in parenting, which so obviously had affected her, but she feared being different, being critical of her parents, going beyond them. She said, "When it was just me, I could allow myself to compromise. I would always say 'No big deal.' But now it's my child, and I can't say it doesn't matter. I don't know what to do. I've got work to do." She told her husband that it was precisely because she was going to be a parent that she would not stop her treatment. As she explained to him, therapy was for the benefit of the whole family.

Beginning and Middle Phases of Treatment

As we have seen, the variety of externalizations in the parent-child relationship is central to work with parents during the beginning and into the middle phases of treatment of children and adolescents. The ways in which we can help parents put aside externalizations lend themselves to techniques for addressing the problem in individual adult patients.

Externalizing Transference

At the beginning of a child's treatment, parental conflict over physical separation from the child often manifests itself in a need to retain control. Externalization is a major mechanism in parents' attempt to control their child's new relationship with the analyst. Similarly, in an adult treatment, the initial transference is often an externalizing one. Externalization is one of the mechanisms of pathological attachment. It is the opposite of attunement (J. Novick and K. K. Novick 1994). The disruption of empathy between parent and child that must be addressed in parent work has direct parallels in problems of establishing the therapeutic alliance with adult patients. Current work on attachment theory, empathic processes in therapy, and right-brain functioning attests to the centrality of these issues and their importance in forming a therapeutic alliance (Schore 2000, 2002). Only after doing the work of sorting out the motivations and current gains from maintaining the externalizing relationship can the treatment proceed to a deeper level.

The push from an adult patient to use externalizations to create (or recreate) a sadomasochistic relationship directly parallels what analysts see operating between parents and children. The important lesson from child work, however, is that these relationships are not one-sided. The initial position of victimization of the child is soon identifiable as a pathological collusion between parent and child. The child plays an active and ongoing role in creating and maintaining a sadomasochistic tie. He clings to the parental externalizations and internalizes them in order to meet important needs and protect primary relationships. The child thereby attempts to stave off panic over object loss and loss of control. Rather than being only the passive victims of adult pathology, children become agents in their own right and bring these patterns into the treatment relationship.

Thus the child analyst deals with a complex web of externalizations and internalizations among and between parents, between parents and children, from parents to the analyst, and from the child to the analyst. Techniques designed to help parents and children first notice, then question, and then examine their externalizations in terms of function are all applicable to work with adults, where we see these mechanisms operating as part of the patient's past experience, recreated in the present treatment.

A young man, Mr. C, had started analysis in a state of despair, not knowing what he wanted in his life. He was pursuing an advanced degree in a field he abhorred, and he was in a relationship with a woman he found repulsive. As he settled into a more congenial line of work and left that relationship, he began to express his disappointment in his analysis. He had started, he said, with the expectation that the analyst would help him decide about his career and his relationships. A whole year had gone by, and only now had he changed work and ended a relationship that had been doomed from the start. Hadn't the analyst seen that? Weren't there techniques he could have used to speed the process and not waste all that time and money?

The next day he said that he was so grateful for the work done; he appreciated the obvious experience and wisdom of the analyst, and he wanted to rearrange his times so that he could continue his analysis despite the demands of his new job. After much effort, a new schedule was arranged, and he promptly told the analyst that he would have to cancel because of work. He didn't think he should have to pay for the missed sessions, despite the clear initial agreement about this. He then began again to express his disappointment in the analysis—he cited all the authorities who claimed that analysis was a waste of time and money. He "could have bought an expensive car for what [he] paid the analyst in the last year!"

This is a difficult, but not so unusual, therapeutic situation. It represents a sadomasochistic impasse, with the potential for stalemate or premature ending, which has tested all clinicians, including Freud. It was in response to the challenge of self-defeating behavior in patients that Freud changed his theory; modern revisions of psychoanalytic theory often arise in opposition to standard theory and technique as attempts to solve such treatment problems.

We suggest that experience with child and adolescent treatment and the kind of parent work we are describing in this book allow for an inclusive psychoanalytic theory and a multimodal technique that can encompass more radical attempts to deal with such clinical challenges. We can apply these ideas to the situation with the patient described above.

With Mr. C, the analyst first focused on what was going on between patient and therapist. The analyst recognized the situation as similar to one in which a parent first idealizes a child, attributing capacities well beyond the child's level of development, then expresses disappointment when the child fails to live up to that standard. The parent feels justified in his indignation that the child has let him down. The analyst interpreted that Mr. C was giving up his own highly developed capacity to make judgments and devise solutions and attributing such powers to the analyst. He was expecting a level of foreknowledge that far exceeded the competence of the therapist. Was this ever done to him? Mr. C responded with old and new memories of being a little boy feeling responsible for his mother's depression, expected to "cure" her and make her happy when even the best psychiatrists were helpless and she had to be hospitalized. In the treatment, he was acting as the abusive parent, externalizing the helplessness of the overwhelmed child onto the analyst, expecting him to perform beyond his capacities and then attacking him for failure to meet the unrealistic expectations.

There were further details as Mr. C and his analyst explored the complexities of the various externalizations and identifications with each of his parents, but the work finally led to understanding Mr. C's childhood establishment of an omnipotent sadomasochistic system to control his relationships. He could elicit high expectations and actively disappoint the other person; through his failures he could gain his own approval to attack the analyst, render him helpless, and end up feeling powerful in his failure. The analyst could use understanding of the dynamics between children and their parents to identify Mr. C's component internal figures of the abusive, externalizing parent; the overwhelmed helpless child; and Mr. C's transformation of his passively experienced trauma into an active construction of a sadomasochistic system of self-regulation, fueled by an omnipotent belief in his power to control others.

Pretermination

Conceptualizing the pretermination phase as a unique period in treatment with specific tasks and conflicts is valuable in general in work with adults as well as in work with children and parents (J. Novick 1997; J. Novick and K. K. Novick 1996b, 2001). From the discussion of parent work during the pretermination phase, we can draw two particular significant applications to individual work with adults. The first is the danger of premature termination at the transition from the middle phase to pretermination. The second concerns various resistances to picking a date and starting the termination phase.

Dangers of Premature Termination under
Pressure from Significant Others

In relation to evaluation, we described how adult patients may use their significant others as objects for externalization of important functions of the internalized parent representations. It is useful to keep this in mind throughout the treatment and to monitor how adult patients are able appropriately to include important people in their lives in the progress of their treatment and development. We have seen that parents who have not been adequately included in work throughout treatment may feel threatened by their child's or adolescent's growing independence and psychological separateness. They may react by ending treatment

163

abruptly in an attempt to return their child to the orbit of a closed system of sadomasochistic control.

In work with adults, the analyst should be alert to intimations that the patient's significant other feels threatened by the patient's increasing self-sufficiency. If the adult patient has not been helped to foster concomitant growth in the partner, the patient may suddenly feel faced with the choice between a summary ending of treatment and the rupture of a marriage or an important relationship. Since the adult patient may also have defensive reasons to avoid the various meanings of leaving, patient and partner may join forces to leave the analyst feeling abandoned, betrayed, and helpless.

> Dr. Y was a highly successful professional who came to analysis profoundly depressed and frustrated with his personal and professional lives. He did not enjoy his work, his children, or his wife. He had been through many alternative treatments, from medication to meditation, with little relief. Psychoanalysis was a desperate last resort, and he commuted an hour each way to attend a very early morning session time. This meant arising before 5 a.m., but he did this without complaint. At first this meshed with his sadomasochistic stance; the suffering that he felt entitled him to be cruel to his family.
>
> In the middle phase of treatment, he found more positive motivations for the deprivation consequent on his session time, as he began to enjoy his work, finding it stimulating and "endlessly fascinating." Treatment began to have major impact on his lifelong passive, masochistic, victimized stance. He increasingly took charge of his own life and initiated major decisions, including ending his loveless marriage.
>
> He began a relationship with a younger woman whom he described as much less educated and sophisticated than he. After a year together, he continued to describe her as someone who brought excitement, fun, and sexual pleasure to his life. Sometimes he slipped into his old sado-masochistic style of relating, but the analytic work had equipped him to counter this pull with assertion and realistic negotiation. Dr. Y felt proud of his newfound capacity to take the initiative at home and at work. Both analyst and patient began to think of what work remained before starting a termination phase.
>
> Then a shift occurred, and the material became sparse; the pleasure and excitement in the analytic work seemed gone. For the first time in years, Dr. Y overslept and began to complain about his commute and the need to wake up so early. Work on his conflicts about ending had some

effect, but it was not consistent and did not feel very genuine. The analyst began to feel helpless as the treatment lost its vitality. The analyst questioned whether something was going on outside the treatment to produce such a change.

Dr. Y then described that he had recently been involved in "nightly orgies" initiated by his girlfriend. They had gone far beyond their usual range of sexual activities. She had introduced a variety of sadomasochistic sexual practices, including role-playing, whipping, bondage, and spanking. Intuitively she had tapped into the patient's continuing battle between his closed-system sadomasochistic solutions to conflict and his hard-won open-system functioning. The patient said, "Doc, we've done great work together, and I'm really grateful, but she has tapped into a side of me that I can't get away from. I'm hooked. It's a rush—like a drug. I can't wait to get home, and I want to stay up all night playing our sexual games. I can't do both—I have to choose. I think we'll have to stop soon."

The analyst and the treatment could not compete with the rush of sexual excitement provided by Dr. Y's partner and the way this interacted with his internal conflicts. Just like parents who cannot tolerate a child's or adolescent's growth and the concomitant shifts in family dynamics, Dr. Y's partner seemed to fear she could not keep up if he kept on changing. Technically, the analyst had missed opportunities throughout the treatment to focus on the importance of involving his partner in his progressive development.

Internalized Conflicts over Growth and Change

In describing the work with Luke's father during the pretermination phase of Luke's treatment, we noted his various difficulties in supporting and enjoying his son's growth. In that situation, there were two separate individuals, each with his own conflicts. If Luke and his father had not been involved in a treatment situation at the critical developmental juncture of Luke's late adolescence, Luke would have internalized some or all of his father's pathological reactions to his progressive changes. If Luke were then seen as an adult in individual treatment, it is likely that he would display serious resistance to change. The techniques we describe in working with parents of child patients can be used to illuminate difficulties, some reaching the dimensions of negative therapeutic reaction, in shifting adult patients from an exclusive reliance on omnipotent sado-masochistic, closed-system methods of self-regulation. What we see in work with parents of children and adolescents applies to the conflicts adult patients experience with internalized parent representations, often externalized onto significant people in their current lives, particularly at moments of transition between phases of treatment.

Termination

The significant other of the adult patient, like the parent of a child in treatment, has had a long, complex, and meaningful psychological relationship with the analyst, even though they usually never meet and it is mediated through the patient. Just as the child analyst is aware that the parent needs to mark the end of the relationship and be helped to mourn, the analyst of the adult has to help the patient see how the ending will impact the significant other. The spouse or other person needs to have feelings acknowledged, both for growth and to be able to support the patient's mourning. Like the actual parent of the child patient, the adult's partner has to acknowledge and work through feelings of disappointment and disillusionment. Only by recognizing the reality limitations of treatment will they be able to accept that the work will continue without the analyst. Finally, just as parents increasingly take on the parental functions initially shared with the analyst—such as validating, appreciating, admiring, and so forth—so the significant other has to be there for the adult patient so that basic human needs can be gratified in a realistic, open, mutual relationship.

CHAPTER ELEVEN
SUMMARY AND FURTHER QUESTIONS

Pragmatic Psychoanalysis

We start from a position of pragmatic psychoanalysis, with the question of therapeutic success or failure foremost. The most obvious measure of success is whether or not the parents of a prospective child or adolescent patient accept or reject the recommendation for treatment. If they and the child accept, we ask whether the child or adolescent can remain in treatment; engage in the necessary work; undergo sufficient positive change; end in a manner satisfactory to patient, parents, and therapist; and retain the positive gains some time after treatment.

Using therapists as their own controls, we have found in ourselves, our colleagues, and our students noticeably greater success on each of these measures after changing our technique to include working with parents. We feel confident in hypothesizing that work with parents through the whole course of treatment will substantively improve therapeutic results. This lends itself to empirical testing, and we would welcome results from any colleagues who would use a sophisticated research design to randomly assign families to therapists who would work with and without ongoing parent work.

In this book we have used a model of therapeutic alliance tasks throughout the course of treatment as a guide or framework. We have discussed our

167

working model and assumptions for parent work. Here is a summary of the main points:

Assumptions

- Parenthood is a normal adult developmental phase.

- Parents and children are involved in a lifelong complex inter-action.

- Analysis of children and adolescents has dual goals:
  Restoration of the child to the path of progressive development;
  Restoration of the parent-child relationship to a lifelong positive resource for both.

- The therapeutic alliance is a conceptual framework for ongoing parent work.

- Treatment has phases.

- There are therapeutic alliance tasks at each phase of treatment for each party to the treatment.

- Child, adolescent, and adult development are continuous; therefore there is a continuum of technique between child and adult treatment.

- Mastery and internalization of the parental therapeutic alliance tasks moves parents through *subphases of parenthood.* This also represents a movement toward greater open-system functioning.

- Parental movement from the "closed" to the "open" system of self-regulation is the overarching criterion of change.

- Parent work is substantive and legitimate. It makes use of the full repertoire of psychoanalytic interventions.

Parents have therapeutic alliance tasks throughout their child's treatment:

- During evaluation, the task for parents is to begin various transformations.

- At the beginning of the child's treatment, parents have the task of allowing the child to "be with" another adult, accepting physical separation.

- In the middle phase, allowing the child to work together privately with another person means integrating the child's psychological separation.

- Enjoying and validating the child's progression is the task for parents in the pretermination phase.

- During termination, parents work to mourn their own loss of the therapy, to internalize mastery of alliance tasks, and to consolidate their own development in the phase of parenthood.

- After treatment has ended, parents allow for continued growth in the child and grow with him.

We have described the tasks of the therapeutic alliance for all partners through the phases of treatment (see table 1) and have made a summary of parental tasks, anxieties, resistances and defenses, and possible interventions (see table 2). As long as we keep in mind that the cells of these tables are not mutually exclusive mechanical checkpoints along the road, but rather that the tables are heuristic devices to describe phenomena that actually persist and overlap throughout treatment, we have found it useful to summarize the issues highlighted in the work of each phase in this form.

Two Systems of Self-Regulation

Throughout this book we have referred to two systems of self-regulation, the open and the closed. Our focus in this book is parent work, and we referred in chapter 2 to our use of assumptions related to the two-systems concept as part of the development of this model of clinical intervention. The underlying ideas, however, may be helpfully spelled out a bit more here, while fuller discussion can be found in papers specifically devoted to the two-systems model (J. Novick and K. K. Novick 2002a, 2003, 2004). We have conceptualized this model in order to make sense of multiple phenomena of development and treatment.

Table I. Therapeutic Alliance Tasks

	Evaluation	Beginning	Middle	Pretermination	Termination	Postermination
Patient	Bring material Engage in transformation tasks	Being with therapist	Working together with therapist	Putting insights into action Independent therapeutic work Maintain progressive momentum	Setting aside omnipotent beliefs Internalization of alliance Mourning	Use alliance skills for living and creativity
Therapist	Initiate transformations of: • self-help to joint work • chaos to order and meaning • fantasies to realistic goals • external complaints to internal conflicts • despair to hope • helplessness to competence • guilt to usable concern	Feeling with patient	Maximum use of ego functions	Allow for patient's independent therapeutic work	Allow patient's mourning Deal with own loss Analyze to end	Stay available as analyst
Parents or Significant Other	Engage in and allow transformations	Allow the "being with"	Allow for individuation or psychological separation	Enjoy and validate progression	Mourning loss of therapy Internalization of alliance Consolidation in phase of parenthood	Allow continued growth Grow with patient

Table 2. Working with Parents Through the Phases of Child and Adolescent Treatment

	Evaluation	Beginning	Middle	Pretermination	Termination
Alliance Tasks for Parents	Engage in transformations	Allow child to be with another	Allow psychological separateness, individuation, autonomy	Enjoy and validate progression	Allow child to mourn Internalize relationship with analyst
Parental Affects/ Anxieties	Guilt, helplessness Failure/mortification Hatred of child Fear of hostility and/or exposure Fear of exclusion	Loss of child Loss of love Guilt over lack of authentic love relationship	Abandonment Loneliness Loss of love Fear of child's assault on parent's personality	Fear of abandonment Sense of uselessness Transference fear of being discarded by analyst	Fear of sadness, love, and loss Fear of reliving core conflicts
Parental Resistances/ Defenses	Externalizing and blaming the child or other factors Push for immediate relief	Various types of externalization	Withdrawal from child Protection of character defenses and superego Resistance to revival and potential revision of past	Preemptive, premature termination—passive to active	Avoidance Premature leaving or withdrawal
Therapist's Techniques, Interventions, and Goals	Acknowledge wish to be a good parent Do as much work as possible through the parents Access primary parental love Clarify contract Differentiate privacy and secrecy Resist urgency	Help parents see child as unique Interpret sadomasochistic relationships	Consolidate parental strengths Interpret past roots of equating loss or death with separateness Reinforce idea that growth is not loss Support reality testing leading to reparation	Do not rationalize a bad good-bye as normal development Address need to learn about parting Support transformation	Acknowledge deep bond between parents and therapist Work until end

In this book we have applied the two-systems model to the theory and technique of parent work. Our ideas relating to potential choices of methods of self-regulation at any point in development have a long history, starting with our early work on two kinds of beating fantasies in children (J. Novick and K. K. Novick 1972). Our continued work on the development of sadomasochism with its core omnipotent beliefs has led us to reclaim for psychoanalysis a dual-track model of development (J. Novick and K. K. Novick 2002a; K. K. Novick and J. Novick 2002c) that allows us to encompass various alternative kinds of self-regulation and conflict resolution. From this we postulated two systems of self-regulation. One system familiar to all analysts in its functioning is the omnipotent sadomasochistic system. We have called this the "closed system" since it avoids and denies reality; is unchanging, circular, and repetitive; and is characterized by static omnipotent sadomasochistic modes of functioning.

The other we have called the "open system" since it is attuned to inner and outer reality; is constantly expanding and changing; and is characterized by joy, competence, and creativity in self-regulation, problem solving, and conflict resolution. These two systems represent alternative potential responses to developmental challenges available to anyone from birth on. Even the most disturbed patient has the potential for open-system responses; even the best-analyzed patient never loses the potential for closed-system responses. At times of stress, such as illness or impending death, it is not unusual to find even very rational individuals turning to omnipotent, magical solutions in religious beliefs or quack medicines.

In previous publications we have applied the idea of two systems of self-regulation to understanding the therapeutic alliance (K. K. Novick and J. Novick 1998), two types of psychoanalytic technique (J. Novick and K. K. Novick 2003), the superego (J. Novick and K. K. Novick 2004), performance (J. Novick and K. K. Novick 1996c), and politics (J. Novick, K. K. Novick, and B. Z. Novick 1997). In this book the two-system model is an underlying assumption and is especially useful in differentiating various concepts central to parent work, for instance, distinguishing guilt from usable concern, externalization from attunement, omnipotence from competence, magic from reality, privacy from secrecy, remorse from regret, and so forth. The alternative choices of types of conflict resolution and self-regulation described in the two-system model are available

throughout development. We have summarized these choices as responses to the ordinary challenges of development at each phase in table
3 below, where we also note signs and symptoms characteristic of solutions within each system.

In chapter 3, we wrote about asking parents to fill out a developmental history form. When the prospective patient is an adolescent, we suggest that parents and adolescent fill it out together. It is a very simple
form, but we have often been asked for a copy, so we are including a recent version at the end of this chapter. The form serves multiple purposes,
and we have found it very useful. It establishes from the outset that the
parents are an important resource for information, and it immediately
shows that the work of evaluation and potential treatment requires cooperation. It conveys our assumption that past development and experiences
may be significant in the current situation, and it opens up the past as a
legitimate arena of inquiry.

We tell parents on the phone as we set up the first meeting that the
information from the form will give us a framework; we can begin to think
of them and their family even before we actually meet. At the first meeting we thank them for returning it before the session (if they have), note
that it gave us some sense of the child's history, and take up any immediate questions arising for them or the therapist from the information provided. Parents often remark spontaneously that filling out the form
reminded them of things they had not thought of for years.

We have described this therapeutic model as a "work in progress." Our
own views have changed greatly since we began to face the enormous failure rate in child and adolescent treatment when work excludes the parents. We hope others can now join us in a more exact and extensive
examination of the obstacles and advantages to working with parents of
children and adolescents through all the phases of treatment.

We have found that another benefit of working with parents is that it
provides a window for examining the phase of psychological parenthood.
Becoming a parent has a unique meaning for each person. This book af-
firms that parent work is a legitimate and coequal therapeutic endeavor
that in turn opens the way to the clinical study of parenthood as a phase
of adult development. What are the components of this phase of adult development? Is there a sequence of subphases, each dependent on the consolidation of a prior subphase? And what cognitive, metacognitive, and

Table 3. Two Systems of Self-Regulation

Phase Challenge	Open, Adaptive, Competent Response	Closed, Omnipotent, Sadomasochistic Response
For Parents during Pregnancy *Parental helplessness regarding physical changes, intactness, and safety of baby*	Helplessness evokes parents' finding areas of realistic effectiveness and sources of support. Conscious planning to avoid repetition of own negative infantile experience.	Helplessness leads to parental fantasy of baby as controller, devourer, savior. Transference to baby from old relationships. Externalization of devalued/feared/wished for aspects of self onto baby.
For Children: **Infancy** *Infant's failure to evoke needed response. Transient parental loss of attunement*	Mismatch followed by repair. This is root of positive feelings of competence, effectance, and reality-based self-regard. Positive feelings instigate and represent effectance and basic object tie. Signs include predominance of positive affect, secure attachment, psychophysiological harmony.	Parent fails child and infant is left in helpless rage, frustration, and traumatic overwhelming. Turn away from reality and competence. Reliance on magical controls. Attachment through pain. Symptoms may include gaze aversion, failure to thrive, hair pulling, head banging, biting.
Toddlerhood *Exploration, independence, and assertion frustrated*	Child's aggression is absorbed in constancy of parental love. Exploration and assertion protected and enjoyed. Autonomy and independence a source of pride, with positive attachment strengthened at new level. Ambivalence can be tolerated with aggression increasingly separated from assertion. Anger and aggressive impulses a useful signal, calling into play ego capacities and realistic use of object. Signs include preponderance of joy, swift recovery from negative affects, capacity to accept help of others and negotiate resolution of conflicts, concern for others.	Assertion defined as aggression, parents helpless to absorb aggression, modulate excitement. Separation experienced as attack. Wishes given stamp of reality—assertion becomes aggression becomes sadism. Self-esteem derived from control of others. Identification with externalizations and externalizing defenses of parents. Symptoms may include rages, sleep disturbances, separation problems, attacking other children, interference with development of speech, toilet mastery, bodily control, mastery of feelings (tantrums, inconsolability).

Stage		
Phallic-Oedipal *Reality of gender and generational differences (exclusion from adult activities)*	Turn to reality gratifications, internal sources of self-esteem. Development of autonomous superego with both affirming and prohibiting characteristics, open to reality corrections. *Signs* include curiosity in service of growing reality sense, development of independent friendships, capacity to use adults as resources.	Child responds to trauma from overwhelming experiences (primal scene, frightening films, TV, etc.) by sexualization, denial, and externalization. Parental collusion with child's wishes promotes formation of omnipotent delusion. Sadomasochistic fantasy organizes superego, which is tyrannical, divorced from reality, unmodified by experience. *Symptoms* include persistence of earlier problems, inability to give up transitional object, bossiness and controlling behavior, provoking attack, obsessional rituals, bedwetting, ego constriction.
Latency *Negotiate rules, rewards, demands, and controls of external world*	Good feelings from image of self as competent, effective, capable of learning, playing, negotiating, socializing, controlling self, and changing. *Signs* include successful mastery of impulses, tolerance of ambivalence, development of complex relationships, capacity for pleasure in work.	Self-esteem based mainly on belief in control of others; Real talents and capacities co-opted to maintain delusional image of omnipotent self (entitlement, exception). *Symptoms* include persistence of earlier problems, intensification of obsessional rituals alternating with wild, "hyper," anxiety-driven behavior, lack of pleasure in real achievements, learning problems, bullying, victimization, inability to play, social isolation.
Adolescence *Real changes in body, mind, and social expectations*	Ownership of mature sexual body. Consolidation of gender identity. Realistic self- and object-representations. *Signs* include pleasure in appearance and functioning of body, increase in capacity to parent self, constant relationships with peers.	Maintenance of omnipotent beliefs by means of increasingly desperate self-destructive actions. *Symptoms* include pathological use of the body (eating disorders, self-mutilation, suicide, substance abuse, pregnancy, repeated abortion, rapid repeat pregnancy, promiscuity), delinquency, depression, fragmentation of personality, low achievement, grandiosity, social isolation.

emotional capacities are needed for the tasks of each subphase? For example, does the capacity to see the child as a separate person predate the experience of attunement and primary parental love, or does it follow from them? Is there a circular feedback in which primary parental love reinforces the capacity to respect and experience separateness?

A further question raised by the sort of parent work described in this book concerns the applicability of the conceptual model of two modes of self-regulation. Is it useful to think of two distinct and irreconcilable modes of parental self-regulation, the "open-system" and "closed-system" types, that coexist as potentials in parenting at all times? For example, is externalization (a closed-system style of defense mechanism) the antithesis of attunement (an open-system way of relating)? Does the use of one inhibit the use of the other? All of the above questions and more remain for further study in which we enthusiastically invite the reader to participate.

Here, in our final chapter, we return to the reason for this book—pragmatic psychoanalysis. Does working with parents in the ways we have described have a significant positive effect on work as a child and adolescent analyst and therapist? It has for us, but the ultimate answer lies with the reader. In this book we have presented illustrations from work with many different families, each of which courageously brought their unique strengths and vulnerabilities, health and pathology, to the situation. We have found that our model of parent work, with its emphasis on developing a working partnership with parents based on mutual respect and trust and tapping into the potential for primary parental love, is effective with even very disturbed families and in extreme circumstances. As therapists, we all share a responsibility to make therapeutic help available to the fullest possible range of families, in as many settings and situations as possible. Being a parent, even under the best of circumstances, is the most complex task that faces adults—everyone can use help and support. Therapists, too, need a model and language for engaging families in the crucial activity of primary prevention and intervention. We have found the elements of our parent-work model indispensable in outreach consultation, in work with the spectrum of families attending the psychoanalytic preschool, and in myriad clinical settings.

We invite others to use this model in therapeutic and outreach efforts and share with us and each other what works, what doesn't, and where future efforts should be directed. Please let us know. We look forward to the comments of working clinicians. It is only by working together that we can fulfill the potential of child and adolescent analysis to transform the lives of children and their families.

E-mail: kerrynov@aol.com or jnovick@umich.edu

DEVELOPMENTAL HISTORY FORM

<u>CONFIDENTIAL</u>

DATE:

CHILD'S NAME:

AGE:

DATE OF BIRTH:

SIBLINGS' NAMES AND DATES OF BIRTH:

PARENTS' NAMES:

AGES:

OCCUPATIONS:

ADDRESS:

PHONE – HOME:

WORK:

E-MAIL:

PARENTS' FAMILIES:

SIGNIFICANT FAMILY MEDICAL AND/OR PSYCHIATRIC HISTORY:

<u>CURRENT FUNCTIONING AND HISTORY</u>

REASON FOR CONSULTATION:

RELATIONSHIP WITH:
MOTHER

FATHER

OTHER ADULTS

SIBLINGS

PEERS

FAVORITE ACTIVITIES, HOBBIES AND INTERESTS:

CHAPTER ELEVEN

PREGNANCY AND BIRTH:

DESCRIPTION OF CHILD AS INFANT:

DESCRIPTION OF CHILD AS TODDLER:

SLEEP:

SELF-CARE, INCLUDING TOILET MASTERY:

EATING:

PLAY:

MILESTONES (SMILING, SITTING, PLAYING, CRAWLING, WALKING, TALKING):

SUMMARY AND FURTHER QUESTIONS

HEALTH:

ACCIDENTS, ILLNESSES, OPERATIONS, HOSPITALIZATIONS:

PRIMARY CARETAKERS:

SEPARATIONS AND LOSSES:

DAY CARE:

NURSERY SCHOOL:

ELEMENTARY SCHOOL:

SECONDARY SCHOOL:

ANY ADDITIONAL INFORMATION:

REFERENCES

Abelin, E. (1975). Some further observation and comments on the earliest role of the father. *International Journal of Psycho-Analysis, 56,* 293–300.

Abelin, E. (1980). Triangulation, the role of the father and the origins of core gender identity during the rapprochement subphase. In R. F. Lax, S. Bach, & J. A. Burland (Eds.), *Rapprochement* (pp. 151–69). New York: Jason Aronson.

Baruch, G. (1997). The impact of parental interventions on the analysis of a 5-year-old boy. *International Journal of Psycho-Analysis, 78,* 913–26.

Benedek, T. (1959). Parenthood as a developmental phase: A contribution to the libido theory. *Journal of the American Psychological Association, 7,* 389–417.

Boelich, W. (1990). *The letters of Sigmund Freud to Eduard Silberstein, 1871–1881.* (A. J. Pomerans, Trans.). Cambridge, MA: Harvard University Press.

Brenner, C. (1985). Some contributions of adult analysis to child analysis. *Psychoanalytic Study of the Child, 40,* 221–34.

Brown, C. (2003). *Good morning midnight: Life and death in the wild.* New York: Riverhead Books.

Burlingham, D., Goldberger, A., & Lussier, A. (1955). Simultaneous analysis of mother and child. *Psychoanalytic Study of the Child, 10,* 165–86.

Burlingham, D. (1973). The preoedipal infant-father relationship. *Psychoanalytic Study of the Child, 28,* 23–42.

Chethik, M. (1989). *Techniques of child therapy.* New York: Guilford Press.

REFERENCES

Committee on Child and Adolescent Analysis. (1997). Unpublished report of the survey of child and adolescent training programs of the American Psychoanalytic Association. Presented by S. Rubin at the Winter Meetings of the American Psychoanalytic Association, New York, December 1997.

DeVito, E., Novick, J., & Novick, K. K. (1994). Cultural interferences with listening to adolescents. *Adolescenza, 3,* 10–14.

Ehrlich, L. (in press). The analyst's reluctance to begin a new analysis. *Journal of the American Psychoanalytic Association.*

Elmhirst, S. I. (1988). The Kleinian setting for child analysis. *International Review of Psycho-Analysis, 15,* 5–12.

Emde, R. (1988a). Development terminable and interminable: I. Innate and motivational factors from infancy. *International Journal of Psycho-Analysis, 69,* 23–42.

Emde, R. (1988b). Development terminable and interminable: II. Recent psychoanalytic theory and therapeutic practices. *International Journal of Psycho-Analysis, 69,* 283–96.

Freud, A. (1965). *The writings of Anna Freud: Vol. 6. Normality and pathology in childhood.* New York: International Universities Press.

Freud, A. (1966). A short history of child analysis. In *The writings of Anna Freud: Vol. 7. Problems of psychoanalytic training, diagnosis & the technique of therapy* (pp. 48–58). New York: International Universities Press. (Original work published 1976)

Freud, A. (1970). Child analysis as a subspecialty of psychoanalysis. In *The writings of Anna Freud: Vol. 7. Problems of psychoanalytic training, diagnosis & the technique of therapy* (pp. 204–219). New York: International Universities Press. (Original work published 1976)

Freud, A. (1980). Preface to *The technique of child psychoanalysis: Discussions with Anna Freud,* by J. Sandler, H. Kennedy, & R. L. Tyson. Cambridge, MA: Harvard University Press.

Freud, S. (1897). Letter to Fliess, Nov. 14, 1897. In J. M. Masson (Ed. and trans.), *The complete letters of Sigmund Freud to Wilhelm Fliess: 1887–1904* (pp. 279–81). Cambridge, MA: Harvard University Press.

Freud, S. (1909). Analysis of a phobia in a five-year-old boy. *Standard Edition, 10,* 3–149.

Freud, S. (1917). Some thoughts on development and regression: Aetiology. In Introductory lectures on psychoanalysis, Part III: General theory of the neuroses. *Standard Edition, 16,* 339–57.

Furman, E. (1957). Treatment of under-fives by way of parents. *Psychoanalytic Study of the Child, 12,* 250–62.

Furman, E. (1969). Treatment via the mother. In R. Furman & A. Katan (Eds.), *The Therapeutic Nursery School* (pp. 64–123). New York: International Universities Press.

Furman, E. (1992). *Toddlers and their mothers.* Madison, CT: International Universities Press.

Furman, E. (1995). Working with and through the parents. *Child Analysis, 6,* 21–42.

Furman, E. (1996). Parenting the hospitalized child: Consulting with child life workers. *Child Analysis, 7,* 88–112.

Furman, E. (1997). On motherhood. *Child Analysis, 8,* 126–49.

Furman, E. (1999). The impact of parental interventions. *International Journal of Psycho-Analysis, 80,* 172.

Furman, R. A., & Katan, A. (1969). *The therapeutic nursery school.* New York: International Universities Press.

George, C., Kaplan, N., & Main, M. (1996). *Adult attachment interview protocol* (3rd ed.). Unpublished manuscript, University of California at Berkeley.

Glenn, J., Sabot L., & Bernstein, J. (1978). The role of the parents in child analysis. In J. Glenn (Ed.), *Child analysis and therapy.* New York: Jason Aronson.

Heller, P. (1990). *A child analysis with Anna Freud.* Madison, CT: International Universities Press.

Hellman, I. (1960). Simultaneous analysis of mother and child. *Psychoanalytic Study of the Child, 15,* 359–77.

Herzog, J. M. (1982). On father hunger: The father's role in the modulation of aggressive drive and fantasy. In S. H. Cath et al. (Eds.), *Father and child: Developmental and clinical perspectives.* Boston: Little Brown.

Hirshfeld, L. (2001). *Work with parents in child analysis and psychotherapy.* Unpublished doctoral dissertation, Center for Psychological Studies, Albany, CA.

REFERENCES

Hurry, A. (1998). Psychoanalysis and developmental therapy. In A. Hurry (Ed.), J. Sandler, & P. Fonagy (Series eds.), *Psychoanalysis and developmental therapy*. London: Karnac Books.

Kris, A. (1981). On giving advice to parents in analysis. *Psychoanalytic Study of the Child, 36*, 151–62.

Leon, I. (1997, November). *How parents are made*. Paper presented at "Children and the Law," Interdisciplinary Forum for Mental Health and Family Law, New York, NY.

Leon, I. (1998). The psychology of reproduction: Pregnancy, parenthood, and parental ties. In J. Sciarra (Ed.), *Gynecology and obstetrics* (Vol. 6, chap. 82). Philadelphia, PA: J. P. Lippincott.

Levy, K. (1960). Simultaneous analysis of a mother and her adolescent daughter: The mother's contribution to the loosening of the infantile object tie. With an introduction by Anna Freud. *Psychoanalytic Study of the Child, 15*, 378–94.

Mahler, M. S., Pine, F., & Bergman, A. (1975). *The psychological birth of the human infant*. New York: Basic Books.

Meissner, W. W. (1996). *The therapeutic alliance*. New Haven: Yale University Press.

Novick, J. (1980). Negative therapeutic motivation and negative therapeutic alliance. *Psychoanalytic Study of the Child, 35*, 299–319.

Novick, J. (1982). Termination: Themes and issues. *Psychoanalytical Inquiry, 2*, 329–65.

Novick, J. (1990). Comments on termination in child, adolescent, and adult analysis. *Psychoanalytical Study of the Child, 45*, 419–36.

Novick, J. (1997). Termination conceivable and inconceivable. *Psychoanalytic Psychology, 14*, 145–62.

Novick, J., & Kelly, K. (1970). Projection and externalization. *Psychoanalytic Study of the Child, 25*, 69–95.

Novick, J., & Novick, K. K. (1972). Beating fantasies in children. *International Journal of Psycho-Analysis, 53*, 237–242.

Novick J., & Novick, K. K. (1994). Externalization as a pathological form of relating: The dynamic underpinnings of abuse. In A. Sugarman et al. (Eds.), *Victims of abuse* (pp. 45–68). New York: International Universities Press.

Novick, J., & Novick, K. K. (1996a). A developmental perspective on omnipotence. *Journal of Clinical Psychoanalysis, 5,* 124–73.

Novick, J., & Novick, K. K. (1996b). *Fearful symmetry: The development and treatment of sadomasochism.* Northvale, NJ: Jason Aronson.

Novick, J., & Novick, K. K. (1996c, October). "I won't dance": A psychoanalytic perspective on interferences with performance. Paper presented at the Lucy Daniels Foundation annual symposium, Cary, NC.

Novick, J., & Novick, K. K. (2000). Love in the therapeutic alliance. *Journal of the American Psychoanalytical Association, 48,* 189–218.

Novick, J., & Novick, K. K. (2001). Parent work in analysis: Children, adolescents, and adults. Part I: The evaluation phase. *Journal of Infant, Child, and Adolescent Psychotherapy, 1,* 55–77.

Novick, J., & Novick, K. K. (2002a). Two systems of self-regulation. *Journal of Psychoanalytic Social Work, 8,* 95–122.

Novick, J., & Novick, K. K. (2002b). Parent work in analysis: Children, adolescents, and adults. Part III: Middle and pre-termination phases of treatment. *Journal of Infant, Child, and Adolescent Psychotherapy, 2,* 17–41.

Novick, J., & Novick, K. K. (2003). Two systems of self-regulation and the differential application of psychoanalytic technique. *American Journal of Psychoanalysis, 63,* 1–19.

Novick, J., & Novick, K. K. (2004). The superego and the two-systems model. *Psychoanalytic Inquiry, 24,* 232–256.

Novick, J., Novick, K. K., & Novick, B. Z. (1997, December). The reality of Hitler and the delusion of omnipotence. Paper presented at the Winter Meetings of the American Psychoanalytic Association, New York, NY.

Novick, K. K. (1988). Childbearing and child-rearing. *Psychoanalytic Inquiry, 8,* 252–60.

Novick, K. K. (1997, August). *What am I going to do in a little canoe: The sequestering of sadomasochism in women's lives.* Paper presented at the annual meeting of Division 39 of the American Psychological Association, Chicago, IL.

Novick, K. K., & Novick, J. (1987). The essence of masochism. *Psychoanalytic Study of the Child, 42,* 353–84.

REFERENCES

Novick, K. K., & Novick, J. (1998). An application of the concept of the therapeutic alliance to sadomasochistic pathology. *Journal of the American Psychoanalytical Association, 46,* 813–46.

Novick, K. K., & Novick, J. (1999). Creativity and compliance. In D. Bassin (Ed.), *Female sexuality* (pp. 63–69). Northvale, NJ: Jason Aronson.

Novick, K. K., & Novick, J. (2002a). Parent work in analysis: Children, adolescents, and adults. Part II: Recommendation, beginning and middle phases of treatment. *Journal of Infant, Child, and Adolescent Psychotherapy, 2,* 1–27.

Novick, K. K., & Novick, J. (2002b). Parent work in analysis: Children, adolescents, and adults. Part IV: Termination and post-termination phases. *Journal of Infant, Child, and Adolescent Psychotherapy, 2,* 43–55.

Novick, K. K., & Novick, J. (2002c). Reclaiming the land. *Psychoanalytic Psychology, 19,* 348–77.

Pick, I., & Segal, H. (1978). Melanie Klein's contribution to child analysis: Theory and technique. In J. Glenn (Ed.), *Child analysis and therapy.* Northvale, NJ: Jason Aronson.

Pruett, K. D. (1985). Oedipal configurations in young father-raised children. *Psychoanalytic Study of the Child, 40,* 435–56.

Pruett, K. D. (1992). Latency development in children of primary nurturing fathers: Eight-year follow-up. *Psychoanalytic Study of the Child, 47,* 85–101.

Rembar, J., Novick, J., & Kalter, N. (1982). Attrition among families of divorce: Patterns in an outpatient psychiatric population. *Journal of the American Academy of Child Psychiatry, 21,* 409–13.

Reza, Y. (1999). *The unexpected man* (C. Hampton, Trans.). New York: Faber and Faber.

Rinsley, D. B. (1981). Borderline psychopathology: The concepts of Masterson and Rinsley and beyond. *Adolescent Psychiatry: Developmental and Clinical Studies, 9,* 259–74.

Rosenbaum, A. (1994). The assessment of parental functioning: A critical process in the evaluation of children for psychoanalysis. *Psychoanalytic Quarterly, 58,* 466–90.

Sandler, J., Kennedy, H., & Tyson, R. L. (1980). *The technique of child psychoanalysis: Discussions with Anna Freud.* Cambridge, MA: Harvard University Press.

Schore, A. N. (2000). Attachment, the right brain, and empathic processes within the therapeutic alliance. *Psychologist Psychoanalyst, 20,* 8–11.

Schore, A. N. (2002). Advances in neuropsychoanalysis, attachment theory, and trauma research: Implications for self psychology. *Psychoanalytic Inquiry, 22,* 433–84.

Shaver, K. G. (1985). *The attribution of blame: Causality, responsibility, and blame-worthiness.* New York: Springer-Verlag.

Siskind, D. (1997). *Working with parents: Establishing the essential alliance in child psychotherapy and consultation.* Northvale, NJ: Jason Aronson.

Sprince, M. (1962). The development of a preoedipal partnership between an adolescent girl and her mother. *Psychoanalytic Study of the Child, 17,* 418–50.

Tahka, V. (1993). *Mind and its treatment: A psychoanalytic approach.* Madison, CT: International Universities Press.

von Hug-Hellmuth, H. (1921). On the technique of child-analysis. *International Journal of Psycho-Analysis, 2,* 287–306.

Warshaw, S. (2000). The contribution of attachment research to my clinical work with parents of school-aged children. *Journal of Infant, Child, and Adolescent Psychotherapy, 1,* 3–17.

Winnicott, D. W. (1949). Hate in the countertransference. Reprinted in D. Goldman (Ed.), *In one's bones: The clinical genius of Winnicott* (pp. 15–24). Northvale, NJ: Jason Aronson.

INDEX